The Five Oddities of The Obama Presidency

J.M. MALIONN

DEDICATION

To my grandfather, the Iconoclast.

To my grandson J.M. whose eyes tell a story full of curiosity and endless potential.

Finally to those who are motivated by high goals and believe that by executing patiently and carefully those goals will be achieved.

CONTENTS

ACKNOWLEDGMENTS

This has been a family effort.
My Grandson J.M. was the focal point of my inspiration.
J.M.'s parents, aunts and uncle shared a significant role in
editing and launching this book.
Grandma was beside me all along, as she's always has.
This book could not have been published without all their
love and contributions.

1 PROLOG

Tuesday, November 22, 2033, 6:53 am

It was two days before Thanksgiving and Grandpa and I had gone out for a walk on a beautiful autumn morning. The air was humid and brisk. The temperature was close to forty degrees, but the sun was shining after a night full of thunderstorms. Our dog Laia was walking a few yards in front of us sniffing every tree and plant while rushing from one to the next. Every cold breath she took resembled a small cloud in the air.

The day of November 22, 2023 marked the 60th anniversary of President John F. Kennedy's assassination. We spent the prior evening watching documentaries and a series of commemorations that left me with plenty of unanswered questions.

"Grandpa, I really liked the stories you told us yesterday about President John F. Kennedy, especially the different theories about the assassin and his handlers."

I enjoyed hearing Grandpa's remarks whenever there was a discussion on relevant events or controversial subjects. I liked how my Grandfather enjoyed making unconventional analysis and remarks that sparked up an interest whenever the same topic was discussed.

My smart watch was a great asset for me. Whenever I anticipated he was going to begin a new conversation on the matter, I would turn on its recorder. This way I can go back and listen to the recordings in efforts to better comprehend his point of view. I wanted to ensure I could recall the facts, and I was pretty sure he did not notice me recording the conversation. Grandpa was 55 when the first smart watch hit the market in 2013, ten years before he retired. Mom used to say that Grandpa had been a techy savvy guy. Though Grandpa did not hesitate to clarify he wasn't any longer by expressing that gadgets had surpassed him a few years ago, and now he's left in the dark.

As he turned to face me, I immediately turned on my watch recorder once again. He asked, "How are you doing with your assignment on the first African American President?"

"I am doing okay Grandpa. Though I'm not convinced I want the title to be 'The first African-American President of the U.S.' I am leaning towards 'The Second Most Important Democratic President in United States History.' What do you think? Do you like the title?"

We continued down the trail. After a few silent strides, he told me, "Why do you think President Obama was not the most relevant Democratic President? Is it because of what you learned yesterday about John F. Kennedy? Is JFK your most relevant Democratic President?"

I stopped and lingered for a while in order to put more thought into his question. But I was naive at the time and was prepared to answer his question, or so I thought.

"No, it is not because of JFK," I said. "I think that President Abraham Lincoln was the most important Democratic President of United States. So that would make President Obama the second most important Democratic leader."

He took a stick from the floor and threw it afar while calling Laia back beside us. Another few silent strides followed and I knew that was a sign he disagreed with my statement, but why?

"I'm sorry J.M., but President Lincoln could have never

been the most important Democrat to become President of the United States, not even the second or the third most important one."

I was really surprised by Grandpa's statement. At ten, I had already studied some U.S. history in school. I knew pretty well that President Lincoln supported the war against secession of the south and fought to free the slaves. He surely had to be one of the key U.S. Democratic Presidents.

As if he was reading my mind, Grandpa said, "Abraham Lincoln was a very important President. He held the United States together under one Federal Government. He abolished slavery and implemented important economic reforms favoring the middle and lower classes. However, Lincoln was not a Democrat as you are assuming."

"No way! You are kidding, aren't you?" We walked a few more strides along the path, then he stopped, turned and stared right into my eyes.

"I am not joking. Abraham Lincoln was a Republican."

"What?" I could not believe what Grandpa was saying. Abraham Lincoln a Republican!

He bent low to pick up a stick from Laia's mouth, stood up and threw it. Laia sprinted towards the stick and Grandpa turned back at me. When he saw my astonishment, he continued talking.

"Let's state the facts, so you understand. The Republican Party was founded in 1854 by abolitionists. Its first slogan was *free labor, free land, free men*. Abraham Lincoln was the Republican Party's first U.S. President elected in November of 1860. One of the most relevant Republican Party objectives was to abolish slavery."

"Awesome!" I uttered. He was smiling, Grandpa enjoyed when he exposed those that reached the wrong conclusion based on conventional wisdom. He was an iconoclast, and liked to provoke with facts that challenged anyone's thinking. He wanted everyone to come up with his or her own conclusions.

"The Democratic Party was pro-slave at that time," he continued. "As a matter of fact, the election of Lincoln signaled the unilateral secession decision of the Southern

States who mostly favored the democratic candidate, Senator Douglas. The main reason being that Democrats wanted to maintain the right to have slaves."

He looked my surprised face and concluded with an unbelievable sentence.

"Most Democrat Presidents before Lincoln owned slaves, though some of them did not bring their slaves to the White House. Although on paper it seemed the Presidents did not own the slaves directly, they did so discretely through their wives and families."

"That's weird! The first African-American President was Barack Obama and he was a Democrat, was he not? How could have Democrats at the time been pro slavery?"

Parties, as with people and cultures, evolve. Democrats evolved to end up defending the rights of minorities'. The two political parties in the United States are full of unconventional and strange facts, facts that people tend to forget and substitute by making assumptions."

"Grandpa, I'd like to learn more about the forgotten and odd facts."

We arrived back home and continued to the backyard, picked up some firewood from the shed and brought it in through the back door. We entered the laundry room and I took a towel to clean Laia's paws.

"If you want J.M., we could talk about Obama's presidency, said Grandpa. In my opinion, President Obama holds the record for the most amount of strange facts in American history. We will call it the Five Oddities of the Obama Presidency."

"What do you mean, Grandpa?" I said. "What are the Five Oddities of the Obama Presidency? Do you think he was not as good as a President?"

He sat on the stole to take off his sneakers and said.

"Do not get me wrong J.M. The fact that Barack Obama was elected marked a big step forward for U.S. democracy. It was a sign of a country maturing. For many people in and outside of the States, Obama's election was a sign of hope. Hope of change, hope of getting out of the economic crisis, of getting the global economy in better shape, hope for the less favored, hope of better opportunities to live the so called 'American Dream'. However, his Presidency delivered good and not so good outcomes. But I do not like to judge because there are always good and bad results. We could talk about the oddities of his presidency though."

"Okay, tell me about these oddities Grandpa."

"Alright J.M. as I previously mentioned, I had put them together in what I like to call the *Five Oddities of the Obama Presidency*. Since it is Thanksgiving and we are going to be busy with preparations, we won't have time to start covering them at all today. However, Grandma and I are staying home for the week. If you finish your homework before dinner everyday next week, we can talk about each one of the five oddities right after dinner. That will cover Monday through Friday, alright? You may use some of it for your paper on Obama."

He threw me one of those glances full of promises that thrilled me.

"Yeah, sure!"

I was pretty sure Grandpa did not care much about black Friday not Cyber Monday. In the U.S., these two days are huge for retailers selling at a discount right after Thanksgiving and it was something that use to drive my aunts and grandma crazy with excitement but not my Grandpa. This meant I would have more of Grandpa's time to myself. A whole week of deep meaningful conversations with my grandfather seemed promising.

Grandpa got up and went into the kitchen. I switched off my watch recorder, only until Monday. It was time to help Mom with the turkey, after all, it was Thanksgiving.

J.M. MALIONN

2. NOBEL PEACE PRIZE AND HUMAN RIGHTS

Monday, November 27, 2023 at 6:30 am

Mom came to my bedroom to wake me up, but I was already awake. "Good morning Mom!"

"Good morning, J.M. Time to start the day," -she approached the window and opened the blackout curtains- "you're awake already?"

"Yeah!!! I'm excited! Today I'll be spending some time with Grandpa, he promised to explain some cool stuff about President Obama."

"OK. You can spend time with Grandpa and listen to his speeches as much as you want, but do not forget the school bus will arrive in less than an hour. Hurry up!"

Through the window, I could see it was going to be a sunny day. It was still dark, but the sky was clear, and the stars were twinkling. A good sign.

I took a shower and put on my jeans and a yellow and green shirt, prepared my school backpack and hurried downstairs. Grandpa was getting ready for his early morning ride on his bike. He had a bottle of water in his hand and an absentminded stare.

"Good morning Grandpa!" -I gave him a kiss- "Remember that today you promised me some of your time

9

for a little while. Are you still planning to tell me about Obama and the Nobel Prize?

"Good morning J.M.," said Grandpa. "That's the idea. I'll review some pieces of information during the day and we'll talk tonight. However, it has to be after you finish your homework. First and foremost."

"Sure, Grandpa. I hope it's interesting. Politics can sometimes be boring."

"Indeed, too much politics is boring. But, I promise you that the issues we are going to discuss tonight are not going to be that boring. I fancy you'll find some unexpected surprises."

"So what is it that we are going to talk about?" I asked.

"We will be covering how odd were some occasions that occurred, considering that Barack Obama received the Nobel Peace Prize a few months after being elected. You will have to wait for the specific details."

Out of the blue, Grandpa changed subjects.

"You see this bottle?" said Grandpa moving towards the kitchen, unscrewing the bottle cap. "What do you think, J.M.? How much does it weight?"

"Couple of ounces, maybe."

"Here, pick it up!"

I extended my arm, took the bottle, and it slipped from my hand. I didn't anticipate it to weigh over a pound. The bottle was full of water, but as it was filled to the top, I didn't see a water mark and didn't realize. The kitchen counter was full with the spilled water. A few drops ran through the surface and spilled on the floor. Our dog Laia was there in a blink of the eye, licking the floor with her long tongue.

Grandpa picked the bottle up and brought a cloth. As we were drying the water and laughing, Mom entered the kitchen.

Grandpa looked up and with his hand signaled her a stop where she stood. Then, he told me, "What happened?"

"You made me think the bottle was empty! I trusted you, but you lied to me."

"I never said the bottle was empty, J.M. You trusted your

instinct based on what you heard and what you saw. I had another bottle near the counter while I was unscrewing the cap off this one. Therefore, you thought it was empty and that I was about to fill it up. You only found out it was full of water after you picked it up. If I still had the bottle in my hand, you would have still been convinced that it was empty. That is what we are going to talk about tonight."

"I don't follow you," I said.

"My talk and body language deluded you into believing the bottle was empty. You just felt the same type of weird misunderstanding and surprises that many people felt regarding human rights and peacemaking during the Obama administration."

Mom interrupted our conversation and said, "Enough, you two! J.M., hurry up!"

"You'll understand tonight. Have a good day at school, J.M.!" Said Grandpa and I finished drying the spilled water with a Cheshire cat grin.

Monday, November 27, 2023 at 8:13 pm

I turned on my watch recorder and selected my Grandpa's voice filter to ensure I could capture everything that night. Then, I called him from my bedroom.

"Grandpa!!! I've finished my homework!"

"Good! Do you want to play Ping-Pong?" Was Grandpa's answer.

I couldn't believe it. He was really getting old. How could he have forgotten about our pending conversations on Obama?

I went downstairs shouting, "Grandma! Grandpa has forgotten about his promise!"

However, when I arrived to the living room, there he was, my grandfather, with his big smile. He was tricking me, again!

"No, J.M., I haven't forgotten, I thought you did. After dinner, you disappeared."

"I had to finish up my homework. Now, I am ready to

learn why you think President Obama is one of the oddest Presidents we ever had."

"I never said he is one of the oddest U.S. Presidents; I said *he has one of the highest records of odd facts among U.S. Presidents.* That doesn't mean he is odd."

"Whatever," I answered.

"Did you read anything about the Nobel Prize over the weekend?" asked Grandpa.

"Of course I did!"

Grandma and I had spent part of Black Friday surfing the Internet. We read the basics about the Nobel Prize, and she explained to me what kind of people usually won it. We read about some of the Peace Nobel Prize Laureates too: Mother Theresa of Calcutta, President Jimmy Carter, and a very interesting South-African named Nelson Mandela. I was amazed by some of the Nobel Prize Laureates' stories. We also read about physicists and doctors that were awarded the Medicine Nobel Prize, and scientists that received the Nobel Prize in Physics.

"So, what it is it you have concluded about the Nobel Prize?" Grandpa asked me.

"What do you mean?" I replied.

"How would you define the winners? Why is a person awarded the Nobel Peace Prize?"

That was an easy question.

"You'd better be old, have done amazing things, be a peacemaker, risked your life defending human rights and things of that nature. But, you better be still alive; otherwise you won't get the Prize nor the recognition."

As I was talking, my Grandpa was smiling, but it was not clear whether he smiled because he agreed or because he didn't. And then, he clarified.

"You are right. However, in some occasions, that wasn't the case. In fact, the Nobel Peace Prize has sometimes been awarded to Organizations instead of people. In the case of President Obama, he was awarded with the Nobel Prize on December 10, 2009, when he was 48 years old. So he wasn't old at all."

I interrupted and said, "So that is the odd fact you

mentioned, Obama was much younger than other winners!"

"Definitely, he was younger," said Grandpa. "When his nomination was announced on October 2009, Barack Obama had been President for only a few months and on his acceptance remarks at the Prize Ceremony in Oslo, he acknowledged he was receiving the Prize because of all he was going to achieve, not because of what he had already accomplished!"

"Weird, isn't it?"

"Yes it is amazing for someone to receive the prize because of his or her future promises, rather than receiving the award based on their past achievements. But that is not what I mean."

Then, Grandpa asked Grandma to look for Obama's acceptance speech. She put on her glasses, reached for her folded screen, and opened up her search engine in less than a minute while simultaneously asking my Dad to turn on the wall screen.

It always amazed me how Grandma was so good with handling all the fancier electronic devices while effortlessly searching for information, and yet she could not figure out how to use the remote control. I did not wait for Dad to turn on the wall screen so I took the remote and did it myself.

"Thanks J.M.," said Grandma. She projected into the wall screen the Nobel Prize website with President's Obama acceptance speech.

Grandpa said, "I love these screens you have now embedded within the wall. And you connect everything. Let's read what Grandma's found." Grandpa was always making comments on our technology, like if he was from a distant planet unknown to me.

Grandma read aloud one of the first paragraphs[1].

---

[1] The Nobel Peace Prize 2009, *"Nobel Lecture by Barack H. Obama,"* The Official Website of the Nobel Prize, Oslo, http://www.nobelprize.org/nobel_prizes/peace/laureates/2009/obama-lecture_en.html (December 10, 2009).

Barack Obama, December 10, 2009: 'And yet I would be remiss if I did not acknowledge the considerable controversy that your generous decision has generated. In part, this is because I am at the beginning, and not the end, of my labors on the world stage. Compared to some of the giants of history who've received this prize -- Schweitzer and King; Marshall and Mandela -- my accomplishments are slight.'

"You're right, J.M.," said Grandma. "I still remember we were all surprised. However, at the time, many of us had high expectations that President Obama would achieve enough success to show in retrospect that he had been rightfully recognized."

"Do you mean he didn't get enough results?" I said. "He didn't start any war, did he?"

"Some would say he supported some of the Middle East civil wars and revolutions like those in Libya and Egypt. Others would argue just the opposite: he didn't do enough to prevent tens of thousands of civilian casualties in places like Syria. But certainly, he did not start any relevant war," answered Grandpa.

"However, as you very well summarized a few minutes ago, to receive such an honor, you should perform remarkably well in one or several areas related to the criteria that is expected of a Nobel Prize winner." Added Dad.

Grandpa continued. "But in areas such as Human Rights, the Obama administration delivered odd surprises."

"What do you mean? Can you give me an example of those surprises?" I asked.

"Sure. There were plenty. Let's start with a very shocking and sad one, Guantanamo."

Today I know what Guantanamo is. Actually, it has become a major topic of discussion at my law school. But on that evening of November 2023, I didn't even know how to spell it. I looked around the living room for any clues on what Grandpa was talking about, but found nothing. As I continued to look, Grandma was glancing over her glasses staring at Grandpa. Mom had that pleasant look on her face which only meant I was in for a good story, and Dad had his poker face on while playing chess on his phone, though he was always fully aware of any conversations in the room.

I asked, "What about Guantanamo?"

"How can I explain it," Grandpa replied, and turning his head towards Mom he asked, "How would you explain to J.M. what Guantanamo was and why it was so relevant?"

"Let me see," answered Mom, "Guantanamo is a city in southeastern Cuba. Its location has been the site of the U.S. naval base since the early 1900's-"

"1903 as per the Cuban-American Treaty," interrupted Grandma. She was already surfing the net. "The United States Naval Station at Guantanamo used to be called Gitmo and did have Navy, Marines, Air Force, Army, and Coast Guard personnel stationed there."

"An American military base in Cuba? Awesome!" I said, "I thought we used to be enemies…"

"That is a whole other topic, J.M. We can talk about Cuba another day, but let your mother finish her explanation of Guantanamo," said Grandpa.

"As I was telling you," continued Mom, "Guantanamo had been a U.S. military base for one hundred years. At the end of 2001, in the middle of the war against international terrorism, President George W. Bush ordered for the establishment of a high security, offshore detention facility where non-U.S. terrorists could be held. The so called *detention center* was built in Guantanamo Bay. The idea being that if the prison were not on U.S. soil, the U.S. would not have to follow international agreements on detention and torture, nor to obey the U.S. constitution. President Bush also ordered that military tribunals would trial the detainees –the standard procedure is to trial them in American courts, where the judiciary standards are higher-. There were many articles, films, declarations, and news about the use of torture to prisoners throughout the Bush years. Those that were released told very scary stories of what was happening inside the prison facility."

"Mom, how on earth did we Americans happen to do

that? What kind of people went there? It does not seem to make sense after what I have learned about our Constitution."

"You are right. Many of us never supported the creation of the detention center at Guantanamo or the kind of treatment given to prisoners. However, countries and politicians react in extreme ways and accept extreme measures after a terrorist attack with 3.000 casualties like the one on September 11, 2001," said Mom.

"OK. I understand. Guantanamo was a freaking prison created by President Bush ...by the way, was he a Democrat?"

"No, he was not. He was Republican."

"Anyway, so what does all this have to do with President Obama? He became President in 2009, eight years later," I asked

"Since 2007, Barack Obama promised he was going to close Guantanamo if he was elected," said Grandpa. "When he finally got elected in November 2008, he reassured he would close it and order to end torture. True to his commitment, as soon as he took office, Obama mandated Guantanamo to be closed within a year."

"So he did the right thing, didn't he?"

"However, the prison was not closed," said Grandpa.

"Wasn't Obama the President? How come his Government didn't obey him?"

"Well, it is not that the Government didn't obey him." Answered Grandpa. "What actually happened is that he changed his mind. Two years later, in 2011 he ordered to continue with the indefinite detention system and requested the restoration of military trials. In the meanwhile, the Obama administration put on hold most prisoner transfers, which in fact, makes it impossible to empty the prison camp and, therefore, impossible to close it."

"Really?" I said.

"I remember it wasn't closed, but with regards to him changing his own original decision ... I didn't remember that!" Said Grandma.

"Why don't we start reviewing what Barack Obama really

committed to, and go from there," said Grandpa. "Grandma, could you look for any information that describes what Obama had promised with regards to Guantanamo and Human Rights before the 2008 elections?"

Mom broke the conversation asking. "Does anyone want some carrot cake? There is some left over from yesterday." And she started to get up from the couch.

"I want!"

That was my sister Alice. Sometimes it wasn't clear whether she was deep in her own world. But when any sweets was offered or any funny proposition was put on the table, she was back on earth in a millisecond.

"Is there any ice-cream left?" Asked Grandma.

Mom nodded, and Grandma added, "If so, I would like to have both, carrot cake and ice-cream please."

Alice, Mom and Grandma had a sweet tooth and would eat almost anything sweet.

Mom went to the kitchen, followed by Alice and Laia.

"So Grandma, what is it Barack Obama promised?" I asked, eagerly to go back to the main conversation.

Grandma was already on her foldable screen. "Here we go, Obama was against Guantanamo very early on, before any presidential campaign had started," said Grandma.

I read on the wall screen[2]:

Barack Obama's Floor Statements, September 27, 2006: 'As a parent, I can also imagine the terror I would feel if one of my family members were rounded up in the middle of the night and sent to Guantanamo without even getting one chance to ask why they were being held and being able to prove their innocence. ... By giving suspects a chance – even one chance – to challenge the terms of their detention in court, to have a judge confirm that the government has detained the right person for the right suspicions, ...'

---

[2] 2006 Congressional Record, Vol. 152, Pg. S10346 (Wednesday, September 27, 2006).

"And of course," she continued, "during the presidential campaign he spoke about his intentions of closing Guantanamo in numerous occasions. Here are some quotes from Obama's campaign."

Barack Obama at San Antonio, Texas, June 24, 2007: 'We're going to close Guantanamo. And we're going to restore habeas corpus. -We're going to lead by example - by not just word, but by deed. That's our vision for the future.'

Obama campaign policy paper, 2008: 'Guantanamo has become a recruiting tool for our enemies. ...The first step to reclaiming America's standing in the world has to be closing this facility. As president, Barack Obama will close the detention facility at Guantanamo.'

Obama campaign website, 2008[3]: 'The legal framework behind Guantanamo has failed completely... Former Secretary of State Colin Powell wants to close it. ....As president, Barack Obama will close the detention facility at Guantanamo. He will reject the Military Commissions Act, which allowed the U.S. to circumvent the Geneva Convention in the handling of detainees.'

"Grandpa, do you need more info?" said Grandma.

"No need," I replied. "I understand Obama hated the Guantanamo detention facility, as he calls it. So, before he became President of the United States, he guaranteed he would close it and give all prisoners a trial under the U.S. laws. Am I right Grandpa?"

"Yeah, a good summary. When he became President, Barack Obama issued an Executive Order to carry out his promise."

---

[3] The Website text remained for several years (campaign website). However, it was removed weeks before this book was published.

"What is an Executive Order?"

Grandma was quick with this one, and we could read it in the wall screen[4]:

CNBC Explains, January 2014: 'Executive orders are as old as the U.S. Constitution itself and usually steeped in controversy.

Every president, from George Washington to Obama, has used them. More than 13,000, in one form or another, have been issued since 1789.

While there is no specific provision in the Constitution that permits them, there is a "grant of executive power" given in Article II of the Constitution.

Presidents have used that language, along with their constitutional powers as commander and chief over the nation's military, to issue executive orders—whether it be to change domestic policy or go to war. And they are legally binding—the U.S. Supreme Court has upheld all but two legal challenges to them (see more on that below).

Most executive orders stem from a president's desire to bypass Congress. The legislative body is not required to approve any executive order, nor can it overturn an order. The best it can do if it doesn't like an executive order is to pass a law to cut funding for the order's implementation. But even then, the president can veto such a defunding law.

The one sure way of getting rid of an executive order is in the White House. If an administration doesn't like an order from a previous president, it can legally reverse it on its own.'

---

[4] "Executive orders coming? Here's how they work," *CNBC Explains*, http://www.cnbc.com/id/101369574 (January 28, 2014).

"Thanks," said Grandpa. "It is good to read the whole text and remember it. Nearly all paragraphs of this description will enlighten our conversations this week."

"Does it mean that President Obama could impose some of his decisions?" I asked.

"Yeah, U.S. Presidents can get their own way, especially in those subjects like the one we are talking about. Let's continue. President Obama issued an Executive Order to get rid of the Bush Executive Order creating the Guantanamo Detention Center. Grandma, I think it will be useful to skim Obama's Executive Order. Could we?"

Grandma was already on it! So we watched at the wall screen text[5]:

Barack Obama Executive Order 13492, January 22, 2009: 'Closure of Guantanamo Detention Facilities

...

Sec. 3. Closure of Detention Facilities at Guantanamo. The detention facilities at Guantanamo for individuals covered by this order shall be closed as soon as practicable, and no later than 1 year from the date of this order. If any individuals covered by this order remain in detention at Guantanamo at the time of closure of those detention facilities, they shall be returned to their home country, released, transferred to a third country, or transferred to another United States detention facility in a manner consistent with law and the national security and foreign policy interests of the United States.

Sec. 7. Military Commissions. The Secretary of Defense shall immediately take steps sufficient to ensure ...no charges are sworn, or referred to a military commission under the Military Commissions Act of

---

[5] The White House, Office of the Press Secretary, *Executive Order 13492*, http://www.whitehouse.gov/the_press_office/ClosureOfGuantanamo DetentionFacilities (January 22, 2009).

2006 and the Rules for Military Commissions, ...and
all proceedings pending in the United States Court of
Military Commission Review, are halted.
BARACK OBAMA
THE WHITE HOUSE,
January 22, 2009.'

Mom was serving plates to everyone, some with carrot
cake, and others with carrot cake and ice-cream. Alice was
also back from the kitchen, sitting on the floor next to the
coffee table where she had placed her plate. Laia sat literally
neck to neck with Alice, her attention was fixed on Alice's
cake.

Grandpa said, "The inauguration of Barack Obama as
the 44th President of the United States took place on
Tuesday, January 20, 2009. That means he was quick in
executing his commitments."

"So, in his second day in Office," he continued,
"President Obama ordered to close the prison, and to
release, transfer, or prosecute the detainees. All should be
carried out in a year."

"I remember he talked at length about getting that task
done. Most had the idea he would see it through, "said
Mom.

"He certainly conveyed that message. Obama received
the Nobel Peace Prize in November 2009, just two months
short of his own deadline for the Guantanamo detention
facility closure. I have his speech here, among the data I
retrieved this morning" said Grandpa. He unfolded some
papers he had printed during the day, he selected one and
read it aloud.

Barack Obama, Nobel Peace Prize Acceptance
Remarks, November 10, 2009[6]: 'And even as we

---

[6] The White House, Office of the Press Secretary, *Remarks by the*
President [Obama] at the Acceptance of the Nobel Peace Prize, Oslo City Hall,
Oslo, Norway, November 10, 2009

confront a vicious adversary that abides by no rules, I believe the United States of America must remain a standard bearer in the conduct of war. That is what makes us different from those whom we fight. That is a source of our strength. That is why I prohibited torture. That is why I ordered the prison at Guantanamo Bay closed.'

'And that is why I have reaffirmed America's commitment to abide by the Geneva Conventions. We lose ourselves when we compromise the very ideals that we fight to defend. (Applause.) And we honor -- we honor those ideals by upholding them not when it's easy, but when it is hard.'

"And what happened on January, 2010? " I asked.

"Let me see. I think I printed some numbers earlier that provide an explanation of what happened overtime ...Here," said Grandpa, "Around 500 prisoners were released from 2002 to 2008, before Obama became President. In January 2009, there were 242 prisoners left at Guantanamo. Around 50 detainees transferred out in the next 12 months. So, there were 190 prisoners by the closing due date imposed by President Obama."

"Barack Obama was the boss, wasn't he? I mean, if you are the President of the United States of America and you give an order to your team, they should follow it or they would be fired or something, I guess."

"Yes, he was the President, and thus, all within his Administration should follow his orders, as long as they are legal. And this one was legal." said Dad, "though, closing the Guantanamo detention center was probably not an easy task considering the time line requested of 12 months."

"Why not? Daddy."

"Despite the specific explanations given by President Obama, I recall that there were few detainees brought to the U.S. for a trial-"

"Only one during 2009," interrupted Grandpa.

"-OK, so if one was transferred to the U.S., there were 189 to be moved to other countries-" Dad commented.

"Or they could be freed." I interrupted.

"No prisoner was left free in the U.S. They would either moved them to other countries as free men or the prisoners had to face trial. The U.S. agreed to the terms of the transfer with other countries though it was not an easy task. Although most countries supported the closure of Guantanamo detention center, almost none wanted to have the detainees transferred to them."

"So Obama's team obeyed his orders; however, it took a bit longer to execute them because of the complexity. Is that what you mean, Daddy? I don't see that to be so strange if the task was so difficult." It didn't seem that it deserved to be added on to the oddities list of Grandpa. Obama wanted Guantanamo closed, he ordered to close it, and he was taking a little longer. Or so I understood from the conversation.

But Dad interrupted my train of thought: "Actually, I think what your Grandpa is going into is that, at the end of the first legislature, that is four years later, Guantanamo detention center was still open with more than a hundred prisoners, aren't you Grandpa?." He paused for a second before finishing his sentence. "I don't know how you call it, but I don't think you can say the President delivered what he promised."

Grandma continued to read from her foldable screen, "There were still nearly 170 prisoners at the end of Obama's first term. That being said, the Obama administration relocated less than 80 prisoners in four years, only 30% of the total number of prisoners he promised to release in less than 12 months, isn't that odd?"

"Laia! Stop!" Said Alice, running around the table.

We all turned to Laia. She was at the other side of the coffee table, her tongue hanging out from her mouth. Her eyes fixed on the remaining piece of Grandpa's cake. She didn't move at all.

Alice was able to grab her and started to pull her by the

neck away from the cake. Her little arms and hands were powerless against a large golden retriever. Pushing with all her power, she couldn't move the dog an inch.

"Laia, that's Grandpa's, not yours," said Alice. "Come with me!" And she pulled harder.

Dad shouted with his demanding voice, "Laia!" And Laia moved away in the direction Alice was pulling.

I heard Alice whispering something in Laia's ear, but I didn't understand. Later in December, when I replayed the conversation I amplified the sound and could hear Alice saying: "Don't worry Laia. I'll give you some. Come with me."

"I saved your cake, Grandpa!" said Alice, with her open, pale hazel eyes smiling with pride.

"Yes you did! Thanks Alice." said Grandpa picking her up on to his lap and kissing her forehead.

Then, he continued. "Though eventually Guantanamo detention center was finally closed[7], the fact that he did not comply with his promises is odd enough," said Grandpa. He stopped to make sure he had our full attention.

He picked his cake, took another bite, looking around the room, and said.

"But what's really odd is that two years after his Executive Order to close the Guantanamo Detention Center, President Obama issued an Executive Order establishing a system to keep the prisoners indefinitely at the facility and to reinstate military tribunals."

"How come! I mean; this is weird. But what is it that he signed? You know that the media sometimes can change the whole story completely around."

Grandma said: "Here you are. This is it."

Barack Obama, Executive Order 13567, March 7, 2011[8]: 'By the authority vested in me as President by

---

[7] This is an assumption by the author. When this manuscript was released for publishing in May 2014, the Detention Center was still open, active and with well over one hundred prisoners

[8] The White House Office of the Press Secretary, *Executive Order 13567*, http://www.whitehouse.gov/the-press-office/2011/03/07/executive-

the Constitution and the laws of the United States of America, including the Authorization for Use of Military Force of September 2001 (AUMF), Public Law 107-40, and in order to ensure that military detention of individuals now held at the U.S. Naval Station, Guantanamo Bay, Cuba (Guantanamo), who were subject to the interagency review under section 4 of Executive Order 13492 of January 22, 2009, continues to be carefully evaluated and justified, consistent with the national security and foreign policy interests of the United States and the interests of justice, I hereby order as follows... .'

"At the beginning of this Order Obama writes *'continues to be carefully evaluated'*. He should say something about the fact that it has not been closed, shouldn't he?" I asked.

"You may be right J.M., at least in conversational terms. However, this is an official document. Let's see what else President Obama signed in his Executive Order. Grandma, could you scroll down?"

Then we could read several paragraphs of which I've summarized here the areas that caught my attention that evening[9].

'Section 1. Scope and Purpose. (a) The periodic review described in section 3 of this order applies only to those detainees held at Guantanamo on the date of this order,

...

(c) In the event detainees covered by this order are transferred from Guantanamo to another U.S. detention facility where they remain in law of war detention, this order shall continue to apply to them....

---

order-periodic-review-individuals-detained-guant-namo-bay-nava (March 7, 2014).
[9] *Executive Order 13567.*

Sec. 2. Standard for Continued Detention. Continued law of war detention is warranted for a detainee subject to the periodic review in section 3 of this order...
Sec. 3. Periodic Review. The Secretary of Defense shall coordinate a process of periodic review of continued law of war detention for each detainee described in section 1(a) of this order. In consultation with the Attorney General, the Secretary of Defense shall issue implementing guidelines governing the process, consistent with the following requirements:
(a) Initial Review. For each detainee, an initial review shall commence as soon as possible but no later than 1 year from the date of this order. The initial review will consist of a hearing before a Periodic Review Board (PRB).'

"Grandpa, If I understand the meaning of all this, President Obama gave the Defense Department around a year to review and act, but there is nothing on going with the prisoners. So, if I am reading this correctly, I gather that there is only a bit of delay with the first order."

"Your observation is interesting. One could conclude up to this point the same as you. However, what happens if the intention is not to free up a detainee? What if at their conclusion the Department of Defense were to continue the detention? Grandma, is there any provision to this effect on the Executive Order?"

Grandma continued scrolling down and we read[10].

'(b) Subsequent Full Review. The continued detention of each detainee shall be subject to subsequent full reviews and hearings by the PRB on a triennial basis. Each subsequent review shall employ the procedures set forth in section 3(a) of this order.'

---

[10] *Executive Order 13567.*

"I see. President Obama ordered that a detainee could stay another three years, another three years, and another three years until they die. Thus, the prisoners continue in Guantanamo prison and, therefore, the prison couldn't be closed. Now I think I understand what you meant Grandpa."

"But who makes the decision for the prisoners to stay at Guantanamo or to be released?" Asked Mom.

"That is a very good question and a key point in all this." Answered Grandpa with a dejected look.

"There are a number of technicalities. But, in essence, the so called military tribunals set up by Bush and criticized by Senator Obama, were brought back by President Obama himself through his Executive Order, avoiding any interference by the House of Representatives. Those same military tribunals were back in charge in deciding the future of prisoners."

"But if those tribunals had already decided that prisoners were to be in prison at Guantanamo, would they change their minds? This in effect, perpetuates Guantanamo until every prisoner dies, doesn't it?"

"The military tribunals could change their minds if and when new information was uncovered. I think that President Obama encouraged the transfer of prisoners to other facilities, this way Guantanamo could be shut down, isn't that the case Grandma? Could you find whether the Executive Order indicated something about this?"

"Is this what you are looking for?" Asked Grandma, scrolling further down on the same document.[11]

'Sec. 4. Effect of Determination to Transfer. (a) If a final determination is made that a detainee does not meet the standard in section 2 of this order, the Secretaries of State and Defense shall be responsible for ensuring that vigorous efforts are undertaken to identify a suitable transfer location for any such detainee, outside

---

[11] *Executive Order 13567.*

of the United States, consistent with the national security and foreign policy interests of the United States and the commitment set forth in section 2242(a) of the Foreign Affairs Reform and Restructuring Act of 1998 (Public Law 105-277).

Sec. 5. Annual Committee Review. (a) The Committee shall conduct an annual review of sufficiency and efficacy of transfer efforts....'

"So there was an opportunity to send prisoners outside Guantanamo, but not to U.S. tribunals. Again, Grandpa, I do not understand."

"Indeed. That is why all this Guantanamo situation is so odd, especially for a person granted with the Nobel Prize." Talking to Grandma, he said. "Could you find any explanation from the Obama administration on the reasons and implications of this Executive Order, Grandma?"

"Let's see. There are a lot of speeches and declarations from the Administration and Barack Obama on the 2009 Executive Order closing Guantanamo, but I can't find any on the decision to maintain Guantanamo open or on the establishment of military tribunals. The Obama administration seemed to want to avoid the issue being discussed," answered Grandma. "There were a few comments on papers, though, maybe these particular ones have what you are looking for."

The Washington Post, March 8, 2011[12]*: 'Obama creates indefinite detention system for prisoners at Guantanamo Bay, Guantanamo Bay trials to resume. President Barack Obama has ordered a resumption of military trials for terror suspects at Guantanamo Bay, in an acknowledgement the prison camp for terror suspect in Cuba is unlikely to close any time soon.*

---

[12] Peter Finn and Anne E. Kornblut, "Obama creates indefinite detention system for prisoners at Guantanamo Bay, Guantanamo Bay trials to resume," *The Washington Post*, March 8, 2011

(March 7)President Obama signed an executive order Monday that will create a formal system of indefinite detention for those held at the U.S. military prison at Guantanamo Bay, Cuba, who continue to pose a significant threat to national security. The administration also said it will start new military commission trials for detainees there.'

CNN, March 8, 2011[13]: 'Obama orders resumption of military commissions at Guantanamo. President Barack Obama announced Monday that the United States will resume using military commissions to prosecute alleged terrorists held at the Guantanamo Bay, Cuba, detention facility.
In the announcement, the president said his administration remains committed to closing the controversial detention facility but will rescind its previous suspension on bringing new charges before military commissions. The commissions are military proceedings rather than trials in civilian courts.'

"And here you have a couple from the more publicly followed TV shows. But that's about it," added Grandma.

Good Morning America, March 8, 2011[14]: 'And an about-face from President Obama on Guantanamo Bay. He is resuming military trials for terrorism suspects held in Cuba, two years after he pledged to close the prison.'

---

[13] The CNN Wire Staff, "Obama orders resumption of military commissions at Guantanamo," *CNN*, http://edition.cnn.com/2011/POLITICS/03/07/obama.guantanamo/ (March 8, 2011).

[14] Juju Chang, *Gooa Morning America*, ABC, March 8, 2011.

Ann Curry and Today, March 8, 2011[15]: 'In a stunning reversal President Obama signed an executive order to resume military trials in Guantanamo, just two years after vowing to close the controversial facility. The order also creates a formal system to keep detainees in prison there indefinitely.'

"Let me see if I understand," I said. "President Barack Obama promised many times over he was closing the Guantanamo prison. He called it a shame for America, and talked about the need to trial the prisoners under the U.S. laws, in U.S. tribunals of Justice. When he begins his term, he issues an Executive Order to close Guantanamo prison in a year and halt military trials. Not one but two years later, the prison is still open and with most of the prisoners in it. He issued another Executive Order resuming military trials and allowing the prison to remain open using a trick."

"Really good, J.M.!" Grandpa congratulated me. "That's a concise summary. Moreover, I believe that most of the detainees that were graded as transferable were not transferred. Let's see if we have any numbers."

Grandpa shuffled through his printed pages and continued.

"Yes, here they are. Two years after the second Executive Order, 50% of about 160 prisoners still at Guantanamo had been cleared for release. Nevertheless, they hadn't left the premises. In fact, I believe that prisoners protested in several occasions because they were neither properly evaluated nor released when they were cleared. I'm sure that was well covered by some foreign media."

"Let me see. There was an article by The Economist published in May, 2013".

The Economist, May 4, 2013[16]: 'The Guantanamo hunger-strike

---

[15] Ann Curry, *Today*, NBC, March 8, 2011

[16] The Guantanamo hunger-strike. The Oubliette, *The Economist, May 4, 2013.*

A desperate protest by prisoners at Guantanamo has shamed Barack Obama

...The protest is a reminder of one of his most glaring failures in office.

Officials count 100 hunger-strikers; lawyers for the detainees say there are 130; on any reckoning, a majority of the 166 remaining inmates are starving themselves. Through their lawyers, detainees complain of a tougher regime since the army took over guard duties from the navy last autumn.

...But the underlying cause is simpler, and more personal. "The reason they're willing to die", says Carlos Warner, a federal defender who represents 11 of the detainees, "is President Obama."

...According to the review, many of these men were low-level fighters rather than total innocents. But none has been charged with a crime—and most have been at Guantanamo for over a decade.'

"You mean...is this true?" I said. "By mid-2013 there were still 166 prisoners waiting for any step forward! The prisoners and their lawyers pointed to Obama".

"I kind of remember the situation had another angle. Obama insisted that Congress was not approving the budget to implement his objective. What really did happen?" asked Dad.

"Actually that was the reason why he initially offered to issue the second Executive Order. However, there are two pieces of data that imply that was not necessarily the case. On one hand, in the first part of 2011 he reinstated the military tribunals he so actively had criticized Bush for. Even though there were many alternative and cheap options that would help trial prisoners the right way. On the other hand, he could have used a presidential waiver to authorize the transfers to cheaper facilities. But he chose not to."

"There were a lot of bipartisan fights, especially in

Obama's second term starting in 2013. And those were frequently used by the Obama administration and the President himself as a disclaimer for their lack of results. However, digging further in the available information, it's easy to realize it was not lack of money. It actually cost the Administration much more to go on with Guantanamo than implementing their initial decisions. Whatever was the reason not to close Guantanamo, it wasn't because bipartisan budget fights."

Then Grandpa rummaged again through his printed notes, took one, and continued. "If prisoners were transferred to the U.S. for prosecution, the U.S. would have saved money. Military tribunals spent $116.13 million just in 2013, based on the Pentagon. The same year, the cost to imprison the 77 men who had been cleared for release was $160 million whereas the cost to imprison that many people in U.S. Federal Prisons would have been $2.6 million according to ACLU, who cites Senate Commissions among other sources[17]. If President Obama wanted to use his powers, he would have saved a few hundred million dollars and obliged with his promises. Why he did not, I didn't know."

"There was also a discussion on whether the U.S. tribunals could judge terrorist suspects, wasn't there?" asked Mom.

"Sure! Some people said that the U.S. judiciary system was not efficient and presented some risks. However, The U.S. civil tribunals prosecuted over 500 terrorist suspects during the period and many were already convicted and are serving their sentences in federal prisons, all following the U.S. laws. I recall this distinctively because Osama Bin Laden's nephew was tried and convicted for cooperation on the 9/11 terrorist attacks on 2013 or 2014. Could we have any of the coverage, Grandma?"

Few seconds later, the wall screen changed to the following text[18].

---

[17] "Guantanamo by the Numbers," Infographics, *ACLU*, https://www.aclu.org/national-security/guantanamo-numbers

The New York Times, March 26, 2014: 'More than a dozen years after the Sept. 11 attacks, a man who came to speak for Osama bin Laden in a series of impassioned videotaped messages that praised the attacks and promised more, was convicted by a federal jury on Wednesday of conspiring to kill Americans and of other terrorism charges.

The defendant, Sulaiman Abu Ghaith, was the most senior Bin Laden confederate to be tried in a civilian court in the United States since Sept. 11, and his swift conviction on all counts would seem to serve as a rejoinder to critics of the Obama administration's efforts to try suspected terrorists in civilian courts, rather than before a military tribunal.

"It was appropriate that this defendant, who publicly rejoiced over the attacks on the World Trade Center, faced trial in the shadow of where those buildings once stood," the United States attorney general, Eric H. Holder Jr., said in a statement.

Citing the success of the civilian courts in "hundreds of other cases involving terrorism defendants," he added, "it would be a good thing for the country if this case has the result of putting that political debate to rest."'

We sat silent reflecting on the numbers brought up by Grandpa and on the Attorney General declarations.

I got up from the couch a bit nervous. What I just heard and read about our recent history was hard to shallow. I was born around those years. President Obama stepped down when I was 4 years old, in January 2017. Barack Obama had been kind of a model for many people, I was told. It is not like we were talking about some old facts of the 20th century.

---

[18] Benjamin Weiser, "Jurors Convict Abu Ghaith, Bin Laden Son-in-Law, in Terror Case," *The New York Times*, March 26, 2014.

Mom asked. "Where is Alice? And Laia?"

Dad called her, "Alice!"

Few seconds later, Alice came through the kitchen door, back to the living room. Laia came a few steps behind, her head low and her tongue licking her lips and nose. Her eyes smiling.

"I'm here Dad. What do you want?" said Alice, sitting on Dad's legs and looking at him with those pale hazel eyes of her and a *good girl* face.

Suspicious was the word that come to my mind.

"What were you two doing at the kitchen?" asked Dad.

"Laia wanted some cake." And she gave him one of her soft smiles.

"But you know she has her own food. You are not supposed to give her sweet food."

"I know chocolate is bad for dogs. They get ill if they eat chocolate. But this was carrot cake and carrots are healthy."

Laia laid down near the TV looking towards Dad and Alice and still liking her nose. Alice cuddled next to Dad.

"Daddy," continued Alice, "I only gave her the leftover crumbs. No one was going to eat the crumbs, and Laia likes them."

"Don't do that again," said Dad. "Before giving Laia any food, ask first, OK?"

Alice always managed to get her way and without being scolded. I was going to protest, ready for battle, when my angry feelings reminded me of our war conversation. So, I went back to the couch asking,

"Grandpa, you haven't mentioned wars and peace. You told us Obama didn't start any war. But there were famous wars at his time, weren't they? Did he end the wars? That would have been a positive achievement."

"You're sharp, J.M.!" said Grandpa. "War and peace is the last part of today's conversations on the Nobel Peace Prize oddity."

Dad was attentive and told me, "I don't know how Grandpa wants to follow the war issues, but just remember that ending a war is not the same as making peace."

"How come ending a war is not making peace, Daddy?"

"I'm sure you'll know why before going to bed tonight."

Mom meddled in our conversation. "J.M., there were two major wars at the time. Both started at the beginning of the 2000s with President Bush, Afghanistan and Iraq."

"Oh, yes." I said. "The news mentions the Afghan war from time to time. What happened? I am sure Obama would have promised to end those wars if he was given the Nobel Peace Prize... or at least he should have promised it after receiving the prize, I guess."

Grandma was again searching online. She started to read[19] , "The ABC archives say that Congress approved the use of force against Iraq on October 2, 2002. On March 19, 2003, President Bush announced the United States would invade Iraq. That is, the war started ten years before you were born, J.M."

I looked at her with a questioning face, and she said.

"Ah, right, you were asking about what Obama promised on the wars.... Let's see. Here you are." And after a few finger strokes on her foldable screen, the wall screen came to light with the following text.

Barack Obama, Fayetteville, NC, March 19, 2008[20]:
'So when I am Commander-in-Chief, I will set a new goal on Day One: I will end this war. Not because politics compels it. Not because our troops cannot bear the burden— as heavy as it is. But because it is the right thing to do for our national security, and it will ultimately make us safer.

In order to end this war responsibly, I will immediately begin to remove our troops from Iraq. We can responsibly remove 1 to 2 combat brigades each month.

---

[19] Anjuli Sastry and Alisa Wiersema, "10-Year Iraq War Timeline", *ABC News timeline*, http://abcnews.go.com/Politics/TheNote/10-year-iraq-war,timeline/story?id=18758663#2 (March 19, 2013).

[20] Remarks of Senator Barack Obama, "The World Beyond Iraq", *Fayetteville, NC*, March 19, 2008.

If we start with the number of brigades we have in Iraq today, we can remove all of them in 16 months. ...What I propose is not – and never has been – a precipitous drawdown. It is instead a detailed and prudent plan that will end a war nearly seven years after it started.'

Barack Obama, The New York Times, July 14, 2008[21] : 'My Plan for Iraq ...That is why, on my first day in office, I would give the military a new mission: ending this war.

As I've said many times, we must be as careful getting out of Iraq as we were careless getting in. We can safely redeploy our combat brigades at a pace that would remove them in 16 months. That would be the summer of 2010 — two years from now, and more than seven years after the war began.'

"And he ended the war, did he?" I said.

"Yes he did," said Grandpa. "It took longer, though."

"Let me find anything about the actual end of the war," said Grandma. "Wait, I have here another announcement, this one after Obama became President. And it seems like a different one."

ABC News, February 27, 2009[22]: 'President Obama made it official today, announcing that he will end U.S. combat operations for the majority U.S. troops in Iraq by Aug. 31, 2010.

Within 18 months, officials expect that 90,000 of the current 142,000 U.S. troops in Iraq will have withdrawn, leaving between 35,000 and 50,000 troops

---

[21] Barack Obama, "Editorial, My Plan for Iraq," *The New York Times*, July 14, 2008.

[22] From Luis Martinez and Z. Byron Wolf, "Obama: 'By Aug. 31, 2010, Combat Mission in Iraq Will End'", *ABC News*, February 27, 2009.

to train, equip and advise Iraqi Security Forces, support the Iraqi government and conduct targeted counterterrorism missions.'

Dad interjected. "You are right. On this declarations, he moved the date to August, 2010. He said he was going to leave between 35.000 and 50.000 troops for training and targeted counterterrorism. Mmmhh. It sounds a bit too many people for training and advice, even if you add the counterterrorism teams. What happened in the end? I kind of remember most of the troops finally withdrew. When did that happen, Grandma?"

"It is a bit confusing," answered Grandma. "It says here that Obama announced the end of the war on August, 2010. But there is some news about the troops leaving Iraq on December 2011. Let me show you."

Think Progress, August 31, 2010[23]: 'Obama Declares an End to Combat Mission in Iraq. President Obama declared an end on Tuesday to the seven-year American combat mission in Iraq, saying that the United States has met its responsibility to that country and that it is now time to turn to pressing problems at home.'

The New York Times, December 15, 2011[24]: 'Almost nine years after the first American tanks began massing on the Iraq border, the Pentagon declared an official end to its mission here.'

ABC News, March 19, 2013[25]: 'In December 2011, after nearly nine years of combat, the last brigades of

---

[23] Special Report, "A timeline of the Iraq War," *Think Progress*, http://thinkprogress.org/report/iraq-timeline/#2009 (August 31, 2010).

[24] Thom Shanker, Michael S. Schmidt and Robert F. Worth, "In Baghdad, Panetta Leads Uneasy Moment of Closure," *The New York Times*, December 15, 2011.

U.S. troops left Iraq, bringing an end to the Iraq War. In its conclusion, the war lasted longer than the Vietnam War and involved more than 1.5 million military personnel. The war also claimed the lives of 4,488 U.S. soldiers and left 32,226 wounded.'

"You are right; it is confusing but for a reason," said Grandpa. "Actually the U.S. participation on the Iraq war ended at the end of 2011. It took twice as much than initially announced by Obama. He made the August, 2010 announcement just to comply with his timings. 2010 was also a midterm election year. He couldn't use the term *end of war*, so he used the expression *end of combat mission*, instead."

"Nevertheless," said Grandma, "the end of U.S. troops in Iraq didn't mean war came to an end, not at all! Unfortunately for the Iraqis."

"I saw a quote this morning," said Grandpa. "Let me see where I have it... This is it! Lily Hamourtziadou said on March, 2014: '11 years on and Iraq is officially at peace. Yet the lines between peace and war have become so blurred that doubt is cast on both past statements and current realities.' Lily Hamourtziadou said this because the monthly death toll during most 2013 and 2014 months was over 1.000 people."

Dad agreed with Grandma and Grandpa's viewpoint. "Peace to the Iraqi soil took many more years to come after the U.S. troops left the country."

"I see." Was my only languid comment.

"What about Afghanistan?" Mom asked.

"When did the Afghan war start and why?" I asked.

Grandpa had the answer in his notes. "One week after the 9/11 terrorist attack to the U.S., President Bush signed a resolution for the use of force against those behind the 9/11 attacks. Three weeks later, the bombings on Afghan soil

---

[25] Anjuli Sastry and Alisa Wiersema, "Final U.S. Troops Leave Iraq, 10-Year Iraq War Timeline," *ABC News*,
http://abcnews.go.com/Politics/TheNote/10-year-iraq-war-timeline/story?id=18758663#16 (March 19, 2013).

began."

"How did they know so quickly that Afghanistan was behind the terrorist attacks of 9/11?" I asked.

"It was well known before the 9/11 attacks that Osama bin Laden, the head of the terrorist group of al-Qaeda and many of al-Qaeda training camps were in Afghanistan. Al-Qaeda was supported by the Afghan Taliban Government. The U.S. Government demanded that the Taliban hand over Osama bin Laden and expelled al-Qaeda. The Taliban requested bin Laden to leave the country, but declined to extradite him or end the support to the terrorist organization." Clarified Dad.

"And did they catch the Al Qaeda terrorists and their heads?" I asked.

"Eventually the U.S. found and killed Osama Bin Laden, the head of al-Qaeda on May, 2011, though not in Afghanistan," said Dad. "But the war was also intended to end with the training camps and the Taliban government, not just with bin Laden. It was quite a complex situation, anyway. You'll study it at school I believe. But let's focus on today's subject. As a candidate, Obama promised to end war in a couple of years, didn't he Grandma?"

"I don't remember. Ah! You want me to search for the information. Ok. Give me a minute." After a few finger strokes, she said, "Yes, Barack Obama made some promises about the Afghan war at the Democratic Convention, in August, 2008," she read aloud, "Barack Obama said, *I will end this war in Iraq responsibly, and finish the fight against al-Qaida and the Taliban in Afghanistan*'."

"And?" I asked.

"Here," said Grandma. "We have a quick, good review of the Afghan war. I think this will sufficient. It's the NBC timeline[26]". We saw a nice timeline picture with the following remarks:

---

[26] U.S. War in Afghanistan, *NBC News*,
http://www.nbcnews.com/id/33210358/ns/world_news-south_and_central_asia/t/us-war-afghanistan/#.U0BEwvl5OSo

February, 17, 2009. 'New President, More Troops. Barack Obama says he'll send 17.000 more troops to Afghanistan, and draw down forces from Iraq'

March 27, 2009. '...He calls for 4.000 more soldiers to train the Afghan army and police.'

December 2, 2009. 'Target: Withdraw by July 2011. President Barack Obama says he want to start withdrawing troops from Afghanistan by July 2011. The President also calls for U.S. 30.000 more troops to be deployed to the country, bringing the total number of troops in the region to 100.000.'

"Yes. Great, he said he would finish the war and then he sent more troops... Maybe, he sent more troops to end with the war quicker. So did he bring the troops back and end the Afghan war?"

"Obama didn't withdraw the troops during 2011 as promised," said Grandpa. "But the Administration reached an agreement to have them out of Afghanistan by the end of 2014. Not all troops were withdrawn, though. Some 10.000 troops remained after 2014."

"CNN's well known journalist Amanpour interviewed NATO Commander on the issue on 2014," said Grandma, signaling a new quote[27].

CNN, April 2, 2014: 'International forces will remain in Afghanistan after the currently scheduled withdrawal at the end of the 2014, NATO's Supreme Allied Commander Europe, General Philip Breedlove, told CNN's Christiane Amanpour on Wednesday.

---

[27] Mick Krever, "NATO Commander: Troops will stay in Afghanistan post-2014," *CNN Blogs*, CNN, http://amanpour.blogs.cnn.com/2014/04/02/nato-commander-troops-will-stay-in-afghanistan-post-2014/ (April 2, 2014).

"I think you will see a very large ISAF combat mission changed to a smaller but continued resolute support, train, advise and assist mission at the end of the year," General Breedlove said, referring to the International Security Assistance Force.

"NATO's mission doesn't end [after 2014]; NATO's combat mission ends, but our train, advise, assist mission begins, and this is very important to remember".'

"The U.S. finally withdrew all its forces at the end of Obama's Administration[28]," concluded Grandpa.

Mom had gone upstairs to help Alice get ready to go to bed and read her a story. The day was ending, and though the Nobel Prize Oddity had been interesting and striking, I was also looking forward to going to bed. Thus, I tried to sum up lessons learned.

"From what we've talked, I gather that, during the Obama administration, the U.S. ended two wars, Afghanistan and Iraq. It took as much as twice the time promised by Obama, but they finally came to closure. Better late than never. However, I was really stunned by all the Guantanamo thing."

I stopped and drank the last sip of water left on my glass. Then, I continued with my summary.

"It was really weird. Let me see if I can recap. First Obama as a candidate shows his despise for the Guantanamo prison. Then, on his second day as President, he announces with trumpets that Guantanamo will be closed in a year. Two years later, Obama reinstated the Bush policy on military tribunals he so much criticized, and created a system by which Guantanamo couldn't be closed until the last prisoner dies in it. And he does this without making

---

[28] This is an assumption. All is pending on negotiations with newly elected Afghan President.

public announcements and while giving speeches about making peace and defending human rights and all that."

After a couple of seconds, I added. "Grandpa I'm happy we decided to have this conversation. This is really odd as you would say."

"J.M. Are you ready to leave it here or do you have five more minutes to talk about the bomb Obama sent while talking about ending the wars?" asked Grandpa.

"A bomb, like Hiroshima? ...I was going up to get ready for bed. But what do you mean by the bomb?"

"Many people didn't know much about it. The Obama administration avoided speaking about the subject during the first four or five years of the Presidency. They classified most of the information as secret."

"So, you are talking about secret bombs? Are these figuratively speaking?" I said.

"No, I am talking about real bombs that killed more than 3.000 people outside war zones, during Obama's Administration."

"Wow! Bombings not in a war. I understand why they wanted to maintain it as a secret!"

"But you are going to bed. We may cover this some other time."

"No way, Grandpa! Make it quick. I want to hear about those secret bombs that killed so many people. You mean the bombings were ordered by President Obama?"

"Many of us assumed that Obama would engage in diplomacy as the main tool to build a new international mood. As President, he called for a new start on relations between the Muslim world and the West based on common interests and mutual understanding and respect.[29] Maybe that was the reason why most never envisioned that his Administration would order more drone bombings than ever outside war countries. Moreover-"

---

[29] "Barack H. Obama - Facts", *Nobelprize.org, Nobel Media AB 2013*, http://www.nobelprize.org/nobel_prizes/peace/laureates/2009/obama-facts.html (November, 2013).

"Drone bombings started under President Bush, didn't they?" Interrupted Dad.

"I think so, Grandma," said Grandpa." I am sure the Wikipedia would have that information under drone bombings or something like that."

"Yes, here it is[30]."

> _Wikipedia:_ _'These strikes were begun by President George W. Bush and have increased substantially under President Barack Obama.[5] Some media refer to the series of attacks as a "drone war".[6][7] Until very recently, the U.S. had officially denied the extent of its policy; in May 2013 it acknowledged for the first time that four U.S. citizens, including Anwar Al-Awlaki, had been killed in the strikes.[8] Surveys have shown that the strikes are deeply unpopular in Pakistan, where they have contributed to a negative perception of the United States.[9]'_

"The relevant subject for the Nobel Peace Prize oddity," said Grandpa, "is the fact that during Obama's Administration drone bombings didn't go down, but up. I got some numbers this morning. The comparison between the Bush five years of drone bombings and the first five years of Obama is quite awesome."

He singled out a page from his notes and read the numbers[31]. "The number of strikes under the Bush Administration was a total of 50 to 52, causing 477 deaths in five years. The number of strikes under the Obama administration accounted to around 325, with 2.374 deaths in five years. A drone bombing occurred every 43 days under Bush's administration, while it was every 4 days under Obama's first two years as a President. Amazing, isn't it?"

---

[30] http://en.wikipedia.org/wiki/Drone_attacks_in_Pakistan.
[31] "Drone Wars Pakistan: Analysis," _New America Foundation_, and "US covert actions in Pakistan, Yemen and Somalia," Bureau _oj Investigative Journalism_, January, 2014 Update.

"And no one said anything? I mean bombed people surely protested," I said.

I yawned and stretched my arms.

"They did protest," answered Grandpa. "Grandma, could you find info on three topics altogether, so we can finish quickly with this point? J.M. should be going to bed anytime soon. His yawn is larger than a lion's one!" Joked Grandpa.

"Sure, what do you need?"

"Something on the protests by U.S. allies on drone strikes in their territories. Any reference to when the Obama administration acknowledged they were ordering these drone bombings. Finally, whether Obama announced the end of such operations or not."

Grandma started to open some windows and look for information in parallel. In the meantime, I said. "Don't worry Grandma. This is as weird as the Guantanamo prison thing. I really want to grasp it."

"Here. Let's see if this is what you need. Pakistan's Prime Minister spoke on the subject here in the U.S.," said Grandma as she projected the following text

Voice of America, October 22, 2013[32]*: 'Pakistani Prime Minister Nawaz Sharif has reiterated his country's demand for an end to U.S. drone strikes inside Pakistan.*

In an address at the U.S. Institute of Peace in Washington Tuesday, Sharif said he wants to see U.S.-Pakistan relations improve "but the issue of drones has become a major irritant in our bilateral relationship."

"The use of drones is not only a continual violation of our territorial integrity but also detrimental to our resolve and efforts at eliminating terrorism from our country," said Sharif.

---

[32] Ayaz Gul, VOA News, *Voice of America*, October 22, 2013, http://www.voanews.com/content/us-accused-of-unlawful-killings-pakistan-drone-strikes/1774276.html

White House Spokesman Jay Carney said the U.S. strongly disagrees with claims that the drone strikes violate international law.

"U.S. counterterrorism operations are precise, they are lawful, and they are effective, and the United States does not take lethal strikes when we or our partners have the ability to capture individual terrorists."'

"I think the first time the Obama administration acknowledged their drone strikes was in April 2012, as per this article," continued Grandma.

The New York Times, April 30, 2012[33]: 'The Obama administration on Monday offered its first extensive explanation of how American officials decide when to use drones to kill suspected terrorists — a tactic that the government often treats as a classified secret even though it is widely known around the world.

"Yes, in full accordance with the law — and in order to prevent terrorist attacks on the United States and to save American lives — the United States government conducts targeted strikes against specific Al Qaeda terrorists, sometimes using remotely piloted aircraft, often referred to publicly as drones," John O. Brennan, President Obama's top counterterrorism adviser, said before the Woodrow Wilson International Center for Scholars.'

"And I don't know if this is OK with you, but I thought it was also interesting," said Grandma showing the following article[34].

---

[33] Charlie Savage, "Top U.S. Security Official Says 'Rigorous Standards' Are Used for Drone Strikes," *The New York Times*, April 30, 2012.
[34] Chris Woods and Christina Lamb, "Drone strikes in Pakistan. CIA tactics in Pakistan include targeting rescuers and funerals," Covert Drone War, Drone strikes in Pakistan, *The Bureau of Investigative*

Drone strikes in Pakistan, February 4, 2012: '*The CIA's drone campaign in Pakistan has killed dozens of civilians who had gone to help rescue victims or were attending funerals, an investigation by the Bureau for the Sunday Times has revealed.*

The findings are published just days after President Obama claimed that the drone campaign in Pakistan was a 'targeted, focused effort' that 'has not caused a huge number of civilian casualties.'

Speaking publicly for the first time on the controversial CIA drone strikes, Obama claimed last week they are used strictly to target terrorists, rejecting what he called 'this perception we're just sending in a whole bunch of strikes willy-nilly'....

But research by the Bureau has found that since Obama took office three years ago, between 282 and 535 civilians have been credibly reported as killed including more than 60 children. A three month investigation including eye witness reports has found evidence that at least 50 civilians were killed in follow-up strikes when they had gone to help victims. More than 20 civilians have also been attacked in deliberate strikes on funerals and mourners. The tactics have been condemned by leading legal experts.

Although the drone attacks were started under the Bush administration in 2004, they have been stepped up enormously under Obama.'

"That's weird. And, even in war, bombing funerals and helpers is disgusting, to say the least!" said Dad.

"It seems that in his fifth year as a President, the

Journalism,
http://www.thebureauinvestigates.com/category/projects/drones/dro
nes-pakistan/ (February 4, 2012).

Administration talked about eliminating the strikes out by 2018," said Grandma.

"2018 was after he finished his presidency. He was promising that someone else would end the drone attacks?" I said

"Let's read what Grandma has on the wall screen[35]," said Dad.

> _The Wall Street Journal, February 5, 2014:_ 'During a visit to Islamabad in August, Secretary of State John Kerry privately told Mr. Sharif that the Obama administration envisioned the CIA program ending within the Pakistani leader's first term in office, said U.S. officials briefed on the discussions. Mr. Sharif's five-year term started in June and ends in 2018.
> Senior U.S. officials characterized the timetable as a "general agreement" within the Obama administration and between the U.S. and Pakistani governments. The White House hasn't set a specific date for when the program would end.'

"So Obama approved ten times more drone bombings than President Bush and he kept it a secret, as Bush did. When pressed, his team said it was all legal and minor. However, more than 3.000 people were killed. And his promise to end the bombing was to be executed by the next President. Amazing!" Said Grandpa.

"I think eventually the bombings were scaled out during his presidency, after some strong pressure," said Dad

"That's right. In his second term, bombings went back more towards the number of Bush's administration bombings. Coincidentally, they took this path under significant pressure from both parties to force the White House to disclose information. That was on his second term

---

[35] Adam Entous, Siobhan Gorman, and Saeed Shah, "U.S. to Curb Pakistan Drone Program, CIA To Target Short List of High-Level Terrorists," _The Wall Street Journal_, Feb. 5, 2014.

and during the 2014 election period; I believe."

"Are you referring to this, Grandpa?" said Grandma sending a new text to the wall screen.

> <u>April 2, 2014</u>: 'Reps. Adam Schiff and Walter Jones Introduce Bipartisan Bill Requiring Annual Reporting on Drone Casualties, April 02, 2014[36]. Washington, DC –Today, Reps. Adam Schiff (D-CA), a member of the House Intelligence Committee, and Walter Jones (R-NC), a member of the House Committee on Armed Services, introduced legislation – the Targeted Lethal Force Transparency Act – to require an annual report on the number of combatants and civilians killed or injured annually by strikes from remotely piloted aircraft, also known as drones.'

"Certainly. It was 2014 then, the sixth year of his presidency."

"Let me finish with a sentence of the announcement of Obama as the 2009 Nobel Peace Prize. It is odd to read it after all we just talked. The Announcement text says 'Only very rarely has a person to the same extent as Obama captured the world's attention and given its people hope for a better future.[37]

After a few silent seconds, he added. "Unfortunately, people had to keep hoping."

I got up deeply affected by that conversation.

It was a long first conversation which would be followed by four more. It was surely one I would not forget.

What an oddity! To use Grandpa's words.

---

[36] Adam Schiff representative official page.
http://schiff.house.gov/press-releases/reps-adam-schiff-and-walter-jones-introduce-bipartisan-bill-requiring-annual-reporting-on-drone-casualties/ (April 2, 2014).

[37] "The Nobel Peace Prize for 2009 - Announcement," *The Official Website of The Nobel Prize: NobelPrize.org.* Press Release at About the Nobel Peace Prize 2009.

3. IMMIGRATION ODDITY

Tuesday, November 28, 2023 at 5:33 am

I woke up in the middle of the night. The room was warm, and I was comfortable in my pajamas and covers. However, the noise of the wind around the house was steadfast and it felt like winter. A door was racketing somewhere in the vicinity.

I listened to the sounds for a couple of minutes. I was a bit scared. You know, I was ten years old, my bedroom was large, and neither my brother nor my sister slept with me in the same room.

Then, I remembered, today was going to be a great day after school. I was going to meet with my schools basketball team -I played the center position in my fifth grade team-. We were going to watch game seven of the the 1994 NBA Playoffs. Mr. Earl Cureton was coming to the school to discuss the game as we watched it. Earl played with the Houston Rockets during the 1993-94 season, and he offered to come, as he did every year when he was around visiting family.

With that in mind, I let the jittery thoughts go, turned around and looked at the alarm clock. The time was five thirty seven a.m. "I am not going to go back to sleep," I said out loud, and I decided to get up and look for some information on the 1994 finals series. I thought it will be good to learn about the game so I could impress my teammates and the trainer.

I got out of the bed, put on my Lakers shirt over my pajamas, took the tablet and went down the stairs to the kitchen. I quietly walked down until I made it to the first floor since I didn't want to wake anyone. Our dog, Laia, heard me coming down. She was looking up towards me from the bottom of the stairs, kind of smiling with her eyes. She conveyed peacefulness. Anyone that has a dog knows what I mean.

I patted her head, told her "let's go to the kitchen!" and switched on the foyer light and the kitchen light as we moved together towards the refrigerator. I left my tablet on the desk, opened the refrigerator and grabbed the milk. Then I took a bowl, poured the milk in and sat at the kitchen table in front of the biscuits my sister cooked with Grandma on Sunday morning. I took one for Laia and a couple more for me.

Comfortable in the warmth of the kitchen, with Laia beside my legs, I started to look up information about game seven of the 1994 NBA finals.

I read the Houston Rockets claimed their first championship in franchise history during the 1994 NBA season, I felt someone over my back and, at the same time, a kiss on my head. I jumped and turned around to discover Dad smiling. "Good morning, J.M. What are you doing up at this time in the morning and with your Lakers shirt?"

"You scared me!" I had been so concentrated that I didn't know how much time had passed. "What time is it, Dad?"

"It's twenty past six. What are you doing? How long have you been awake?"

"I woke up and decided to look into the 1994 NBA Finals. Today Earl Cureton will be visiting the school, and all the basketball players and coaches will meet to watch this game. Mr. Cureton will be discussing what happens all along the projection. We can ask him questions at the end. I am reading about the game, so I can put together some smart questions."

"Good. But at what time is this going to happen? After class?"

"Yes."

"Have you spoken with Mom or myself to plan how you are going to come back tonight?"

I felt ashamed. I had forgotten to ask my friend for a ride home and I did not tell Mom or Dad. When I was going to answer, Grandpa entered the kitchen and said, "Good morning everyone! Hey J.M., what are you doing in here? Finishing your homework in the early morning?"

"No, Grandpa." And I began to share my plans for later this evening with my basketball team.

Then, Dad told Grandpa: "Grandpa, what are your plans this evening? Could you or Grandma pick up J.M. at the school after they watch the game? I won't be able to be there, and J.M. forgot to ask Mom or some friends for a ride."

"Sure! I'll be happy to," Grandpa answered. "At what time would be appropriate?"

"Five thirty will be OK. Do we meet at the gym door?" I asked.

"Sure, I'll be there, maybe with Grandma," said Grandpa while taking a seat. "Would you make me a cup of coffee, please?" he asked Dad. Then he looked to me and said: "So, J.M., are you going to have time for another Oddity of the Obama Presidency? You are probably going to be busy after dinner."

"I will not have so much time as I did yesterday nor tomorrow. But you mentioned there are five Oddities. And we need to talk every day about one of them if we want to finish by Friday. Is there a way we can take less time?"

Grandpa gulped down half his cup of coffee while looking through the window. "I was thinking on taking the bike and doing some exercise, but it seems there is some nasty winds out there. I will probably stay home and play with your little brother, Hector."

"Yes, J.M." he continued. "There is one that wouldn't take much time. We'll talk about it tonight."

"What is it about?" I asked.

"It is about immigration. A scorching and controversial issue at the time. The Obama administration really stunned everyone when most of the public realized what had been happening for over five years under his watch. I am sure your Dad will agree it was astonishing when people realized what the Administration was still doing in 2014."

"Indeed," answered Dad. "I do remember pretty well. It certainly was amazing!. I agree it counts as a big oddity of the Obama Presidency"-he looked at me-"that is when I learned the word *Snollygoster*."

"*Snollygoster*? What does it mean?" I asked Dad.

"*Snollygoster* means something like a clever, unscrupulous person," answered Dad. "That's what my boss said about Obama when he discovered what the Obama administration was doing. Keep in mind that my boss was born in Mexico."

"Snollygoster.... Sounds like a little weird word and a bad one for a President. Why did he call Obama such thing?" I said.

Dad sipped his coffee and said, "Let's leave the immigration subject for tonight. Meanwhile, enjoy the game this afternoon. The struggle of Hakeem Olajuwon Vs Patrick Ewing had its climax at the seventh game. Let me know what you think after you watch it, J.M."

"Sure, Dad. I'm going upstairs to get ready for school." I gave Dad a kiss, as he also was getting ready to go to work, and went upstairs, already thinking about the game we were going to watch after school.

However, while I was getting dressed, I remained intrigued by the issue of immigration. What could the Obama administration have done on that issue? How could immigration become one of the Five Oddities of the Obama Presidency? And did President Obama deserved the *snollygoster* name?

Tuesday, November 28, 2023 at 6:48 pm

Mom had prepared one of my favorite dinners with her slow-cooker: roasted lamb leg. She cooked the lamb with garlic and rosemary, and she served it with baked potatoes and green asparagus. The lamb was one of my preferred dishes, and I liked baked potatoes, but did not like asparagus at all.

"J.M., could you pass me your plate?" asked Mom.

"Sure, Mom!" and I handed her my plate. "But no asparagus, please."

"J.M., you know you have to eat any food we serve," said Mom, with a harsh look.

I objected. "But you know I don't like green asparagus."

"I have served you just two," said Mom. "Here you have your plate. And please do not put that face."

Dad was smiling, and he said: "J.M., don't exaggerate and don't put that face. You know, your face reminds me of the face I had at the end of the finals game you watched this evening. I wanted the NY Knights to win. But they didn't."

"How was the game?" he said. "How did you like the performance of Hakeem Olajuwon?."

"Mr Cureton said that Olajuwon outscored Patrick Ewing in all seven games. In his opinion, the Rockets would not have won if it were not for his total domination. He said that the Knicks had one of the best defensive teams of all time. I really liked watching him play. I wished I could play just as good as him."

"He was right. Olajuwon's performance was unquestionably historic. Did you have the opportunity to ask any questions to Earl Cureton?"

"I asked him about the rebounds of Charles Oakley. He was impressive! I didn't know that he played his last season with the Houston Rockets."

"I didn't know that either," said Dad.

"Yes, he played the 1994 NBA Playoffs with the NY Knicks against the Houston Rockets. Ten years later he played his last game with the Houston Rockets." I was proud of what I knew.

"Ah. That is quite similar to one of the Senators or Congressmen during all the immigration projects in the

2000s with Bush and Obama. He was Republican, then he moved to the Democratic Party. I can't recall his name or whether he was a Congressman or a Senator, but he was one of the relevant immigration law advocates." I learned later that Grandpa was talking about Senator Arlen Specter[38].

"Grandpa, what is it about this Immigration Oddity? Why don't you tell us about it just after dinner? I've got a little homework, so I can finish it afterwards. And you said it was going to be striking but short."

"J.M., the agreement with your Grandpa was that he talks about the oddities after you finish your homework," Mom told me.

"But, Mom, I prefer to do it now. Could we?"

"I promise to keep it short," said Grandpa. "And I'll make sure that J.M. finishes his homework before going to bed."

"OK, but just for today," said Mom.

When we had finished dinner, I helped put away the dishes, while Dad fixed everything in the dishwasher. Mom offered some ice-cream and Grandma helped her to serve it. We took them to the living room, and I sat on the floor near Dad's chair.

"So Grandpa, are you going to tell us?"

"Sure!" he answered, while serving himself ice-cream.

Grandma handed Grandpa a napkin, saying: "Clean your chin. Your ice-cream is all over your mouth and dripping."

My sister was laughing. "Grandpa, you don't know how to eat icecream," she said. "Hector does it better!"

Grandpa was a little embarrassed. My sister was right. Grandpa didn't know how to eat soup, icecream or any other meals worthy of a spoon.

Grandpa took the napkin, cleaned his mouth and chin and said, "We will follow the same scheme as yesterday. First we review the promises based on which Senator Obama was elected President of the United States. Then, we review what

---

[38] Arlen Specter, United States Senator from Pennsylvania. Specter was a Democrat from 1951 to 1965, then a Republican from 1965 until 2009, when he switched back to the Democratic Party.

steps his Administration took to fulfill his promises and what happened. In the end, we'll see if it all seems odd enough to put immigration in the list as one of the Five Oddities of the Obama Presidency, OK?"

"So what did he promise?" I asked

"Before we start, I think we need a brief introduction of the immigration situation in 2007-2008," said Grandpa. "The U.S. is a country built by immigration. Most people that came over the years were from Europe at the beginning-"

"I know about immigrants and all that Grandpa. I have visited Ellis Island in New York," I interrupted.

"As your Grandpa was saying, this is a country of immigrants. What we saw at Ellis Island was only part of the story," said Dad. "Immigrants have come over to the U.S. in many waves over the years, some earlier than Ellis Island, others after it."

"Go on," said Grandpa to Dad. "You'll probably summarize the situation better and quicker than me."

"Anyway," continued Dad. "Though most of the immigration waves came from Europe, in the late nineteen hundreds and early two thousand there was a continuous inflow of immigrants from Latin America and to a less extent, from Asia. Many of those Immigrants entered the U.S. illegally and worked in the U.S. without becoming legal immigrants."

"But if they were illegal, how could they work?" I asked.

"They did not have working permits," explained Dad. "But, usually, the employer and employee would agree on a job and salary, and then the employer would pay the employee without making any official statements or declaration to Social Security or the IRS."

"To add to what your Grandpa was saying," continued Dad, "I think there were around 12 million illegal immigrants in the U.S. at the time, of which probably around 80% were Latin Americans. There were also around thirty five million legal immigrants living in the U.S. In the early two thousand, before Barack Obama became President, between seven hundred thousand to eight hundred thousand people entered illegally in the United States every year. Also, every year, over three hundred and fifty thousand of illegal immigrants living in the U.S. become legal immigrants. Additionally, between six hundred thousand to seven hundred thousand immigrants came legally to live or work in the U.S. Of course, these are numbers that changed during the economic crisis of 2007."

Dad was reading the numbers from some web page via his phone.

"J.M., did you understand all the gibberish numbers?" asked Mom.

"I think so," I answered. "Every year, 1.4 million people arrived to the U.S. from abroad. Eight hundred thousand came illegally and six hundred thousand did arrived legally. Illegal immigrants grew by less than half a million because nearly four hundred thousand illegal immigrants managed to become legal every year."

"Very good, J.M.," said Grandpa. "You have your parents' math abilities. I am impressed! I think it is interesting to look at the trends before and after the Barack Obama administration. Do you have information of the Pew Research Grandma? They have been the reference for immigration data since I can remember."

"Pew Research you said? Let's see. Here you are. This is a nice graph from their webpage."

Grandma projected a curve of total unauthorized immigrants in the U.S., starting the count in 1990. But before anyone could discuss the curve, my sister asked:

"Mom, may I have more icecream, please?" Mom was starting to say no with her head, but my sister insisted: "yes Mom, please, please, please... J.M., tell Mom we all want more icecream, please."

I looked to Grandma with my best smile, and she said: "I would have a bit more also, would you mind if I serve a bit more to the children?"

Mom reluctantly agreed, and Grandma went to the kitchen for more icecream, followed by my sister who took my bowl with her. I went back to the curve on the wall screen, and saw Grandpa doing some calculations.

Grandpa told Dad, "the year before Barack Obama was elected President, there were 12.2 million *unauthorized immigrants* as per this Pew Research. The number increased around half a million a year since 1995. Look at what they said in 2013[39]: '*Since 1990, the nation's unauthorized immigrant population has more than tripled*'"

"The curve shows the number of illegal immigrants going down after 2007," I said.

"Good observation, J.M. At the end of the first term of President Obama, Pew Research estimates the number of illegal immigrants in at 11.7 Million."

"And how did President Obama manage to reduce the number of illegal immigrants living in the U.S.? Did he legalize them, Grandpa?"

"That is a good question," said Dad. "I assume that is part of what Grandpa wants to talk about, isn't it?"

"Yes, it is. The economic crisis that started in 2007 was one of the reasons why the number of illegal immigrants dropped after 2007. As unemployment grew the number of illegal immigrants coming to the U.S. looking for a job decreased. However, there are other factors introduced by the Obama administration that made this immigration issue such an oddity. But let's continue to take it one step at a time," said Grandpa.

"You were going to talk about Obama's promises," I said.

Grandma arrived with my sister from the kitchen and the icecream bowls. They passed them around, and I took mine.

"At that point in time, eighty percent of illegal immigrants were of Spanish origin. And around 8% of voters in the 2008 elections were Spanish voters," said Grandpa.

I was more attentive to the icecream than to Grandpa's words, so Dad clarified what Grandpa was trying to convey: "What Grandpa means is that there was a need for a solution towards the illegal immigrants in this country, as no

---

[39] "U.S. Unauthorized Immigration Population Trends", 1990-2012. *Pew Research*, September 23, 2013.

country should have so many illegal people, and growing. Also, if any candidate had an attractive proposal, he or she would be supported by the Latino voters, as the Hispanic community would benefit the most by any immigration solution."

"I am sure that at that time candidate Barack Obama meant what he promised, but he and his team were also aware of the power of those promises to attract the Hispanic vote," interjected Grandma.

"But which were Barack Obama's promises?" I asked.

Mom intervened, saying, "candidate Barack Obama said during his campaign that he would give illegal immigrants a path to citizenship."

"Do you mean that the 12 million illegal citizens were going to become citizens of the United States? Is that what Obama proposed?"

"Right. He promised that most illegal immigrants would eventually get the U.S. citizenship. However, it was not going to happen right away, and it was going to require effort on the side of the immigrants. Grandma, could you look for couple of instances in which Barack Obama publicly explained what he proposed?"

Grandma was savoring her icecream with pleasure. "Sure," she said. She took her time leaving aside her bowl and picking up her foldable screen. Unfolding it, Grandma asked: "You want Barack Obama quotes on the immigration issue?"

We knew it was a rhetorical question, so Grandpa did not respond, but waited. Once Grandma was on the foldable screen, she was quick, and in a few seconds we were watching two quotes on the wall screen[40].

Barack Obama, 2007: 'We've got to give a pathway to citizenship. But people have to earn it. They're going to have to pay a fine. They've got to make sure that they're learning English. They've got to go to the back of the

---

[40] Barack Obama Speech at Chicago, Aug. 8, 2007.

line so that they're not rewarded for having broken the law.'

Barack Obama, 2008[41]: 'We need comprehensive reform ... We have to require that undocumented workers, who are provided a pathway to citizenship, not only learn English, pay back taxes and pay a significant fine, but also that they're going to the back of the line, so that they are not getting citizenship before those who have applied legally.'

"I see," I said. "What happened?"

"During the first term he did not pass any new piece of legislation," said Grandpa[42].

"But Grandpa, if he did not pass any legislation, did Hispanic voters vote him for reelection?"

"Actually, during the 2012 campaign I think he passed a small piece of law that gave most Hispanics the expectation that he would deliver his promises on his second term. Grandma, can you find it for us? Any immigration laws passed in 2012."

Grandma moved her fingers once again, and in a little while she showed Grandpa a paragraph. "Is this what you want?"

"Oh, yes. It was an Executive Order. Do you recall Executive Orders J.M.? We talked about it yesterday."

Grandma projected the webpage she had showed Grandpa.

"Sure. I do remember. They are a kind of law that the President can issue by himself without Congressional or Senate approval, right?"

"Indeed. As you can read on the wall screen, President Obama issued an Executive Order to halt deportations and

---

[41] Barack Obama, during a debate in Austin, Feb. 21, 2008.
[42] Congressmen and Senators introduced several versions of DREAM Act since 2001. The bill was reintroduced in 2009 to the Senate by five Democrats, two Republicans and one Independent Senator

legalize illegal young immigrants under a number of restrictions."

And we read.

ABC News, June, 2012[43]: 'President Obama announced today that his administration would stop deporting and begin granting work permits to hundreds of thousands of young illegal immigrants, saying the changes would make the nation's immigration system "more efficient, more fair and more just."

... The executive order, effective immediately, applies to illegal immigrants who were brought to the U.S. before they turned 16 but are younger than 30, have been in the country for at least five consecutive years, are in school or have graduated from high school or earned a GED, have no criminal history or have served in the military.'

Once I understood what Grandpa meant, I said: "You mean that his first attainment happened almost four years after being elected President and it was taken during the reelection campaign?"

"Certainly," answered Grandpa. "President Obama issued the Executive Order on June 15; that's four and a half months before the 2012 Presidential elections. During the first half of 2012, the expectations of being reelected weren't that good for Mr. Obama."

"That was a very political move to attract Latin and Asian votes. Didn't Hispanic voters realize that? Did President Obama sustain the same support from Hispanics in his second election?" Mom was saying, when Grandma interrupted her.

"Yes, it was a political move, but voters don't care as far as they get what they want. Look at what the New York Times said about this movement[44]."

---

[43] Mary Bruce, "Obama Says Limiting Deportations Is 'More Fair and More Just," *ABC News*, June 15, 2012.

The New York Times, June, 2012: '... they [Latino voters] said they welcomed his move, whatever his motivation. "We know this is political — we like that it's political," said Robert Meza, a Democratic state senator from Phoenix. "People are smart enough to know that of course it's politics, but if their agenda moves forward, they're happy.'

"Politically based decisions are quite frequent during election periods and, though it may not be the most ethical thing to do, U.S. Presidents take advantage of their positions to make decisions that would enhance their chances to get them re-elected," said Dad.

"But the point I want to make is that he waited four years to take a step in the direction of his promises. Until that point, he was saying he did not have the power to do anything, including the fact that he could not order what he actually did in the Executive Order. That was odd and unpleasant, and some Latino leaders reflected on it afterwards. Do you have something Grandma?"

"There is an article on the issue." And she changed the contents of the wall screen to show a Wall Street Journal article:

The Wall Street Journal, February, 2014[45]: 'In November [2013], Mr. Obama, responding to a heckler at an event in San Francisco, said, "If, in fact, I could solve all these problems without passing laws in Congress, then I would do so."

---

[44] Helene Cooper and Trip Gabriel, "Obama's Announcement Seizes Initiative and Puts Pressure on Romney," *The New York Times*, June 15, 2012.

[45] Laura Meckler "Immigration Impasse Could Rekindle Fight Over Deportations, House's Retreat on Legislation Puts Obama Administration in a Tight Spot,' *The Wall Street Journal*, Feb. 7, 2014.

He gave a less definitive response a week ago ..., "I'm going to look at all options to make sure that we have a rational, smart system of immigration."

Advocates note that in 2012, the Obama administration suspended deportations of many young people who were brought to the U.S. as children. Before doing that, administration officials said they didn't have authority to do so.'

I reflected on what I was reading, and after a minute re-reading it again I understood and said: "That is quite odd. The President saying he can't do something and later he does it. Either he didn't know what his power was, or he didn't want to act for whatever reason."

"We'll get to the reason later, as it is also quite strange. But this is just a minor oddity within the immigration issue."

"I agree that wasn't very sincere. But Grandpa, I kind of remember there was also a relevant factor on the immigration issue. Wasn't it true that the Congress was dominated by Republicans, and the Republican majority didn't want to accept Obama's law proposals? I mean, if the Republicans didn't vote for the bills Democrats proposed, President Obama couldn't get the laws passed."

"You are right to a certain point. I remember that was the argument President Obama gave for most of his unaccomplished objectives, not just for immigration. He managed to convey the message that it was all the Republicans' fault. However, the information was not entirely truthful. First, many Presidents have had Congress or Senate dominated by the other party, and they managed to negotiate and pass consensus laws. But second and more important is the fact that both Congress and Senate had a Democratic majority for two years. If the Obama administration or the Democrats had gotten the initiative in those two years, they would have managed their way and could have passed the immigration law they promised. But they didn't propose the law until Obama's second term. Also, some Democratic Senators and Congressmen didn't support the way the Obama administration was managing the immigration issue."

Grandma told Grandpa: "As I was looking around for the Executive Order, I came to an article mentioning something related to your argument. Let me see if I can get it again. Yes, here it is."

The Economist, February, 2014[46]: 'As A presidential candidate in 2008, Barack Obama promised to enact immigration reform during his first year in office. Although his party controlled both arms of Congress for the next two years, he barely tried.'

"That is a strong accusation," I said.

"Indeed," said Dad. "But The Economist is a liberal magazine. It strongly supported Obama's proposals during his candidacy to President. So, I guess it was not an accusation to take lightly. If they thought President Obama barely tried to enact immigration reform, they were probably right."

"Actually," Grandma continued saying, "I think I also had seen a comment about when the Democrats proposed a major piece of law on the immigration subject. Let me see. Here you are. But, it wasn't until 2013, so the initiative to implement Obama's immigration proposal did not happen until his second term at the White House." And she projected the following text that Mom read aloud.

Business Insider, January, 2014[47]: 'Last year [2013], the Senate passed an immigration bill that included a 13-year path to citizenship for undocumented immigrants, increased spending on border security, a beefed up E-verify system, a quicker path to citizenship

---

[46] R.G. and A.M., Daily chart, "Obama and aliens," *The Economist*, February 7, 2014.

[47] Danny Vinik, "Immigration Reform The Two Big Questions - On Immigration Reform," *Business Insider*, January 27, 2014.

*for   DREAMers,   and   increased   high-skilled
immigration.*

*Speaker John Boehner (R-Ohio) has said that the
House will not take up a comprehensive bill like what
passed the Senate. Instead, the lower chamber will pass
a series of smaller bills.*

*The administration has previously said that any
immigration bill must include a pathway to citizenship.'*

"So did they manage to get that law approved during
Obama's second term? Or what?" Was my reaction to what
I just read.

"No, they didn't. Actually that is what this Business
Insider's comment is about. But you know, the strange thing
is that many Democrats and Republicans shared similar
principles for immigration policy. The only diverging one
was that President Obama insisted in the fact that the only
acceptable law had to include a path to citizenship for the
twelve million immigrants as we just read, while Republicans
wanted to give them a legal status equivalent to the legal
status of any other legal immigrant."

Dad asked, "Grandpa, are you sure they were based on
same principles but the citizenship one?"

"I may be wrong, but I believe that was the case. I am
sure there are Internet sites summarizing both the bill
proposed by the Republican President George W. Bush, and
the one proposed in the second legislature of Obama.
Grandma are you on it?"

"This isn't that easy. There are a lot of things about a
DREAM law proposed by the Bush Administration and later
by the Obama administration. However, there is not that
many talking about what you asked me."

My sister was sleeping alongside me with the dog. I
called the dog, "Laia come here with me, and let me pet
you." Laia got up slowly not to disturb my sister and came to
lay by my side. Then, Grandma found what Grandpa had
asked for.

"I have found the four principles of what the White

House called *'principles for a common sense proposal'*. Here you go." And Grandma projected the four principles.

The White House web, 2014[48]: 'There are four principles to the President's common sense proposal:

- *Continuing strengthening border security.*
- *Streamlining Legal Immigration.*
- *Earned Citizenship.*
- *Cracking Down on Employers Hiring Undocumented Workers.'*

Grandma continued. "And here are the principles of the bill promoted by President George W. Bush, Obama's Republican predecessor. I didn't find a similar summary. But these are four sentences of the Senate bill proposal, ordered in the same manner than the previous summary[49]."

- *'Would require specific improvements in border security.*
- *Temporary-worker program would be created.*
- *Would bring undocumented workers already in the United States out of the shadows... in order to obtain what would be known as a "Z visa."*
- *Would establish a strong employer verification system.'*

While I was reading and comparing both summaries, Mom asked Grandpa: "So the difference was just on whether the illegal immigrants were going to be granted residency or citizenship? It doesn't matter one way or the other as far as illegal immigrants are legalized and get working permits, social security numbers and so on, does

---

[48] The White House Web, Issues, Immigration as of March 2014.
[49] U.S. Senate, *S. 1348 – Secure Borders, Economic Opportunity and Immigration Reform Act of 2007*,
http://www.justice.gov/archive/olp/pdf/s1348sap.pdf (May 23, 2007).

it?"

It looked like Dad had finished his latest set of online chess matches, as he was wholly attentive to the discussion and searching the web, as well. He projected a text on the wall screen and said.

"I agree with you. If I am an illegal immigrant that came to the U.S., of course I would want the most I could get. But I would be more than satisfied if I got a permanent visa, working permit and legal status. And that was the sentiment of the illegal immigrants at that time, as recorded by Pew Research. Look at what they got in their survey:"

The Pew Research, December, 2013[50]: 'The Pew Research surveys asked Hispanic adults and Asian-American adults which, in their view, is more important for unauthorized immigrants currently living in the U.S.: "being able to live and work in the U.S. legally without the threat of being deported" or "having a pathway to citizenship for those who meet certain requirements."

Among Hispanics … 61% say being able to live and work in the U.S. without the threat of deportation is more important for unauthorized immigrant than having a pathway to citizenship. Meanwhile, just 27% say the opposite—that a pathway to citizenship is more important.'

"J.M., you may be asking yourself if illegal immigrants thought that way, then why bother to fight for the citizenship part of the law proposal?" asked Mom.

She answered her question right away.

"There is a great difference for politicians, though not for immigrants. If the immigrants get citizenship, they have the right to vote. And of course, the potential votes to one

---

50 Mark Hugo Lopez, Paul Taylor, Cary Funk and Ana Gonzalez-Barrera, "Views about Unauthorized Immigrants and Deportation Worries," *Pew Research*, December 18, 2013.

or another party are very relevant to politicians. Democrats wanted the immigrants to be citizens so they could vote. This was under the assumption that most Latino immigrants would mostly vote for Democrats. Republicans wanted to avoid any citizenship process, so as to ensure the number of Democrat voters didn't increase."

"But if Obama could get 90% of his immigration electoral promise," said Grandma, "why not to agree on a law that could be attractive to a number of Republicans and Democrats alike? Even if that means giving legal status and work permits instead of pushing for citizenship? I mean, it will be more than enough to satisfy most illegal immigrants' desires. Why would Obama insist on his terms and never pass a comprehensive law when he could have agreed on one just as good?"

"I couldn't agree more with your arguments. However, you would have to ask him yourself. I can only speculate," answered Grandpa.

Dad was nodding while looking into his phone, and said: "I also remember that there was a strong debate about the fact that Republicans wanted to increase the border budget and other enforcement activities. From what we read a minute ago, it seems both President Bush and Obama wanted to increase border security. Nevertheless, how much money is devoted to enforcement could be a great obstacle before reaching any agreement. What do you say about that Grandpa?"

"That is a very good observation. You could reduce the number of illegals by giving them legal status, better border protection and deporting those illegals that were living in the U.S.. The last two actions cost a lot of money. Democrats and Republicans were discussing money and were accusing each other of being irresponsible for not coming to terms. However, the reality was that Obama deported more people than any other President in the U.S.. While Obama was accusing Republicans of being the cause for the suffering of immigrants, he was contributing to the largest deportation in history"

"I remember deportations were an issue. But are you

sure about that strong statement, largest deportation in history?" asked Dad. "That would really be odd. A President that promises to pass laws to alleviate the Immigration problem led the Administration that deported more illegal immigrants than any other President in the U.S.?"

I looked towards Grandma to see if she was searching for info that supported Grandpa's argument. What he was saying sounded pretty unbelievable.

"Yes, I'm sure," answered Grandpa. "That is why immigration received the questionable honor to be one of the Five Oddities of the Obama Presidency, because the record deportations of the Obama administration."

"There is a long article in The Economist, published in 2014 on the subject. It is entitled *Barack Obama, deporter-in-chief*," said Grandma.

"Deporter-in-chief?" I said. "Those are strong words."

Grandma was already projecting the article on the wall screen.

The Economist, February, 2014[51]: 'Barack Obama, deporter-in-chief - America is expelling illegal immigrants at nine times the rate of 20 years ago; nearly 2m so far under Barack Obama, easily outpacing any previous president. Border patrol agents no longer just patrol the border; they scour the country for illegals to eject. The deportation machine costs more than all other areas of federal criminal law-enforcement combined. It tears families apart and impoverishes America.'

Dad was reading The Economist issue on his phone and added some points. "The Economist issue has a lot of information in different articles around the same issue. And look at what it says about the money argument!. It seems that President Obama spent more on the deportation

---

[51] Immigration, "Barack Obama, deporter-in-chief, Expelling record numbers of immigrants is a costly way to make America less dynamic," *The Economist*, February 8, 2014.

machine than one would assume. The so-called *Immigration and Customs Enforcement* (ICE) had its own air operations. They flew 6 charter flights a day in 2013. Detention centers and flights alone should have cost a lot of money! And look at what it says here: *'More than half of all federal prosecutions are now for immigration-related offences'*, and here: *'In the two years to September 2012, 205,000 parents were deported'*. Amazing"

Dad continued reading his cell phone and added: "Read this section." And he projected another section of The Economist.

The Economist, February, 2014[52]: 'The data that are collected, combined with estimates to fill the gaps, suggest that in the past couple of years, for the first time since people started to talk about illegal migration, the outflow has been greater than the inflow.'

It seemed that what Grandpa had said about the fact that Obama deported so many people got all the family's attention. Grandma was also reading her foldable screen, when she said: "It seems it wasn't only prestigious liberal journals, like The Economist. Also, the most significant Latino leaders called President Obama the deporter-in-chief. Here is what Janet Murguia, President of the National Council of La Raza, said in her speech[53]."

Janet Murguia, March, 2014: 'For us, this president has been the deporter-in-chief - Any day now, this Administration will reach the two million mark for deportations. It is a staggering number that far outstrips any of his predecessors and leaves behind it a wake of devastation for families across America....

---

52 Leaders, "Barack Obama has presided over one of the largest peacetime outflows of people in America's history," *The Economist*, February 8, 2014.
53 Janet Murguia, President and CEO, NCLR, "Capital Awards Speech: President's Message," *NLCR Capital Awards*, at Washington, DC, March 4, 2014.

...One out of every four deportees is the parent of a child who is a U.S. citizen. Hundreds of thousands of these children, our children, are being deprived of their mother or father— and very often the family's only breadwinner. It will take generations to heal the harm caused by inaction.'

We all read in silence both The Economist paragraphs and Janet Murguia speech. I think everyone was trying to digest the information we just read. But I did not understand why President Obama led the greatest deportation machine in U.S. history, a machine that cost a lot of money.

I had to ask. "But, Grandpa, why a Democratic President that has promised to take care of immigrants and resolve the illegal immigration problem would be in charge of an Administration that does such horrendous things?"

"I do not know. As I told you, I can only speculate," Grandpa answered.

"You do not have to speculate. The same issue of The Economist had a paragraph on its article that has an answer for you:"

The Economist, February, 2014[54]: Why would a supposedly liberal president oversee something so illiberal, cruel and pointless? The Machiavellian explanation is that it motivates Latinos, who associate such barbarism with Republicans, to keep voting for the Democrats.

My sister was sleeping on the couch. My little brother was upstairs sleeping. I was caressing the dog. The rest of the family was deep in their thought.

I interrupted the silence.

---

[54] Immigration, "Barack Obama, deporter-in-chief, Expelling record numbers of immigrants is a costly way to make America less dynamic," *The Economist*, Feb 8th 2014.

"Grandpa. Yesterday we talked about the oddity of the Nobel Prize. I was surprised that the Obama administration didn't live up to the Nobel Prize he just received. But I think this is more odd than what we talked about yesterday. An ugly oddity I would say."

"So, how would you summarize the immigration oddity of the Obama Presidency, J.M.?" asked Mom.

I continued caressing the dog trying to summarize what I had learned in the last hour. My parents and grandparents waited to hear my answer. I took my time and, then, told Grandpa.

"When Obama was a candidate, he promised he was going to solve the immigration problem that was growing year after year. But, when he could have passed a law, he didn't propose any. On the contrary, he waited till the next election to announce an Executive Order to solve a minimum problem. A problem he previously said he had no authority to solve. That would be the first part.

"The second part is that the main difference between the 2007 Republican initiative of President Bush and the 2013 Democratic initiatives was pretty similar in all but one subject: whether the immigrants were going to be legalized or to be awarded citizenship. But it was something the immigrants didn't really care about. It was a political move that favored one party more than the other. So they didn't agree and thus they didn't pass a law.

"And the third one is the most important and amazing thing. While all these discussions about the lack of legal initiatives, the Obama administration was deporting more people than any other, without talking about it. And it wasn't because there were more illegals than before. In the first graph, we saw that the number of illegal immigrants was 12.2 million when President Obama was campaigning and less than 12 million while he was President. Grandma just showed that there were more deportations than immigrants arriving illegally to the U.S.. And, finally, to deport so many people, the Obama administration spent a lot of money they could have used for better purposes."

"Good summary, J.M.," said Grandpa. He gave me a

high-five!

I knew it was time to do my homework, but I did not want to. I was very comfortable talking with the adults and getting their answers to my questions and comments. However, Dad looked towards my direction, and I said: "OK, Dad, I know. I have to go upstairs and finish my homework. I'm going."

"I haven't said anything, J.M.," said Dad. "But you are right, you should go to your room to finish your homework."

I got up and left my bowl in the dishwasher before heading upstairs.

4. JOBS AND THE ECONOMY

Wednesday, November 29, 2023 at 2:57 pm

"What time is it, J.M.?" Asked Ann Marie. It was the fourth time she asked me something during science class today. It bothered me. Ann Marie sat behind me and was a pain in the neck. My best friend, Ethan, insisted she had a crush on me. But I didn't care. I didn't like her.

I turned around, glared at her with an angry face, and said "stop it!" a little too loud. She smiled, her cheeks blushing. I insisted. "Ann Marie, stop pushing me in class!"

I felt Miss Moore walking over towards us before I could see her. "You two, stop interrupting my class with your chatter, please!" she said. Thank God, the bell rang. Miss Moore turned around quickly and finished her homework instructions, as students were getting ready to leave. It was our last class for the day.

I ran out of class with Ethan, away from Ann Marie.

Today was a warm day, the sun was shining. My anger calmed as we walked towards the parking lot. I liked Wednesdays. We usually had little homework and Mom used to pick us up since she didn't work on Wednesday afternoons.

Mom was by her car, in a red coat and wearing a beautiful dress. She was talking with other moms.

"Hi Mom!" I yelled running towards her. Mom smiled with that beautiful, peaceful smile of hers as she waited for me to arrive.

"How was your day, J.M.?" she said giving me a kiss.

I looked back at the school door and saw Miss Moore with Miss Hightoes in deep conversation. Fortunate for me, Miss Moore would not have the chance to talk with Mom and tell her about the incident that happened in class.

"Visual and Performing class was fun today. We had to act on conveying the meaning of a sentence the teacher was reading. We could not talk, and we had to improvise. I liked it," I said.

"Good," said Mom. Then she addressed her friends. "I'm leaving. I have my parents at home. See you next week."

My sister Alice called through the car window, "J.M., your girlfriend Ann Marie is calling you."

I opened the car door and jumped in, saying, "Come on Mom! Let's go!" And to my sister, "She is not my girlfriend!"

"Why not J.M.? She is so pretty. And she likes you." That was Alice, too naive. Instantly she changed subjects. "I learn how to spell cattle, c, a, t, t, l, e. What did you learn at school today?"

I answered "You know... I think yesterday's conversation on immigration was pretty cool because-"

"That conversation was boring," interjected Alice

"You are a kid Alice. But I'm not. That was a serious conversation for grown-ups." I wouldn't challenge my own believe that 10 years of age was the onset of adulthood. A lack of judgment on my side due to my inability to grasp the reality. Later, I found out how much a fool I was. Recently I discovered how many adults make a fool of themselves by not looking around challenging their own assumptions with reality.

Oblivious to our discussion, Mom asked, "Why did you say it was good to talk about immigration yesterday?"

"Because we had a very interesting class exercise," I said. "We had to map the different colonies of Maryland, New Amsterdam, New Jersey, Pennsylvania, and Delaware. Did you know that Manhattan was called New Amsterdam and was the capital of New Netherlands?"

"Interesting, isn't it?" said Mom. "Why did you have to map the colonies?"

"We had to map them and learn about the wide variety of ethnic, linguistic, and religious groups that settled during the first hundred years of the U.S. history. English, Dutch, Swedish, German and Irish settled in that area. Can you imagine? At that time, anyone coming for opportunities, work and freedom to practice their religion could come and stay. It was just the opposite of the massive deportations by Obama's Administration we talked about yesterday."

I stopped talking and after a minute, I asked, "Mom, does the U.S. Government still deport as many people today as did the Obama administration?"

"No, J.M. The following Presidents have managed to implement some solutions."

"I see," I said and stayed silent looking through the window, absentminded.

When we arrived home, I jumped out of the car, yelling, "Grandma, Grandpa!" as I walked inside.

There was a spicy, sweet smell in the air mixed with the living room's flowers fragrance. Music was coming out of the kitchen. It sounded like Grandma had some old music from the eighties and Grandpa was singing along.

I left my backpack on the floor next to the stairs and ran to the kitchen. I stopped at the entrance. Grandpa was mimicking a singer named Kenny Rogers and singing, "... *And youuuuu decorated my life, created a world where dreams are apart. And youuuu decorated my life by painting your love all over my heart... You decorated my life."*

I started to laugh at this scene. Grandpa mimicking Kenny Rogers while Grandma finished cooking some Lebanese cakes and took care of something else in the kitchen. Grandma was staring conspicuously at him.

Grandpa was such a bad singer, but he acted as if he had a great voice even though he knew he didn't.

Alice passed by running towards Grandpa. Grandpa grabbed her and gave her a big kiss. Then, he came to the door and gave me a high-five. He liked to say 'Hi' to me that way.

"What are you laughing at, J.M.?" said Grandpa. Although already he knew.

"Why do you sing, Grandpa? You are so bad at it!" I asked him.

"I like how you sing, Grandpa," said Alice. "You look happy and it's beautiful when you sing to Grandma. It shows you are in love with her."

"Thanks, Alice. Yes, I love your Grandma," answered Grandpa. Then looking at me he said, "I sing because *I can*." He said these last words with a distinctive tone.

I did not understand why the sudden tone. So I looked back at him with a questioning glare.

"*Yes, I can!*" he said, with the same intonation and a mischievous grin.

I was going to ask him what was he talking about when Mom entered the kitchen saying, "J.M., Alice, go upstairs to clean your hands and come back down to eat your snack. J.M., pick up your backpack and take it to your room."

I left the question for later. I was hungry and looking forward to Grandma's homemade sweets.

When I went back to the Kitchen, Alice was telling Grandma, "Grandma, I love you coming to see us. Your cooking is bananas. I like your recipes from around the world. Where are these ones from?"

"They are Lebanese," I jumped in.

"They resemble Lebanese and Jordanian pastries because they are made with almonds, honey and sesame. But these are Andalusian, from Spain. They are called *Pestinhos* and *Tortas de Aceite*. Come here and sit. Here you are." And she gave me a Pestinhos.

Most Wednesday afternoons we sat with Mom in the kitchen after school and ate a snack together. She liked to sit with us and talk. It was great.

After the conversation on Tuesday evening, I was eager to learn about the topic of the next oddity. So, I tried to bring up the subject.

I said, "Grandpa, can we continue our conversation on Obama's Presidency?

Grandpa answered with a grin. "*Yes we can.*" I didn't know whether he was smiling or starting to laugh.

"Are you joking with me?" I said.

"No, J.M."

"Then, what's so funny?"

"Grandpa's got a very personal sense of humor, an ironic sense of humor," said Mom. "He's using one of the most well-known Obama slogans, *Yes We Can*, aren't you, Dad?"

"Right," said Grandpa. "It was a slogan that conveyed hope and raised expectations that people would be able to achieve what they couldn't get before Barack Obama. He intended to relay that message, under his presidency, many people and the U.S. could leap from an adverse situation to the economic and social stand that could not have been achieved in the past or could not be achieved with other candidates."

Grandma added, "The first achievement being that an African-American managed to be elected President of the United States of America. That in itself was a symbol of what could be accomplished."

"OK, But what is so funny ...or ironic?" I insisted.

"Candidate Obama's message had several edges. One of them was the economic one. The U.S. sustained a severe economic crisis starting in 2007. When President Obama was elected, the economic crisis was at its peak. It was a time in which many people lost their jobs. That together with the idea that everyone had to have his or her opportunity for a better life and that the promise that wealth would be better distributed summarized into a message: *Yes we can* have a better live, *yes we can* get back our jobs, and *yes we can* reduce poverty and improve living standards."

"That is a very positive message not a funny one."

"Certainly. It is not a funny one. It ended up being ironic though," said Grandpa with a grin. "Let me use Obama's words. I was looking for some info this morning and I got this quote coming from his BarackObama.com page-"

I interrupted. "He had his own webpage with his name? How cool!" I said.

"- the quote is not from his campaign, but from a moment later in time, but it was basically summarizing what Barack Obama meant by the *Yes we can* on economy and jobs." And Grandpa started to read from his old tablet[55]

> *Barack Obama, Organizing for Action: 'A strong economy starts with a strong middle class. But for too long, increasing inequality and decreasing economic mobility have posed a fundamental threat to the basic bargain of America—that if you work hard and play by the rules, you can build a better life for you and your family. That's why we need to preserve the American Dream by ensuring every American has access to good-paying jobs, the opportunity to own a home, and a quality education.'*

"So what's the irony Grandpa?"

"Voters believed the slogan, and hoped it would become true. And, eventually, part of it became true."

After a few seconds, he got serious and continued. "My answer to you is *yes we can* talk about the third oddity. But me saying we can doesn't mean we can talk about it now as you may have inferred."

And with that argument he changed gears and started to talk with Mom about something else.

I took a bite to my Pestinhos and thought to myself where could the irony be. But I had to trust Grandpa and wait till tonight.

---

[55] Barack Obama's web page, Get The Facts, Issues: Jobs & Economy, *'Organizing for Action,'* http://www.barackobama.com/economy/ (March 27, 2014).

Wednesday, November 29, 2023 at 7:48 pm

Dinner was great. The spicy aroma I detected when we arrived from school was curry. The main course was curry turkey. Warm, yellowish, a bit hot, with rice and raisins. Mouthwatering.

After dinner, I brushed my teeth and went to the living room. Grandpa was sitting on the floor playing and laughing with my little brother, Hector. Alice was petting Laia, both of them laying on the floor half asleep, in a bundle of golden hair. Grandma had a Pestinhos, eating it in small bites.

I threw myself onto the couch and saw that the wall screen was on and with the following text[56]:

Barack Obama, November 10, 2007: 'I'm in this race for the same reason that I fought for jobs for the jobless and hope for the hopeless on the streets of Chicago...
... That's why I'm running, Democrats -- to keep the American Dream alive for those who still hunger for opportunity, who still thirst for equality.'

"What's this text? I thought we were going to talk about the slogan *Yes we can*. That's the third one of The Five Oddities of The Obama Presidency, right?" I said aloud.

"Actually, we won't talk about the slogan," said Grandpa. "The subject of the oddity is the economy, and specifically jobs, wages, income inequality, and poverty. What you have in front of you is the paragraph that sums up the message of hope on the economic expectations delivered by the Obama campaign."

"Anyone wants some tea or coffee?" Asked Mom as she entered the living room.

Only Grandma answered. She asked for some green tea.

I read the text again. "So this was written by Barack Obama?" I asked.

"Not written but spoken." Answered Grandpa. "This is a

---

[56] Barack Obama, Speech in Des Moines, IA, November 10, 2007.

text of a famous speech given by Barack Obama at Des Moines in 2007. But the same message was conveyed in many of his speeches and debates. It was a message of hope in the middle of the 2007 economic crisis. It wasn't just the poorest or the immigrants that lost their jobs. Jobs were slashed all around the country and abroad."

"Was it like last year's crisis? Mom and Dad talked about the economic crisis that started last year. Some of my friends' dads and moms have lost their jobs," I said.

"Kind of," said Dad as he was taking a seat on his favorite chair. "However, the unemployment rate in 2022 topped at 8.7%, and it has been improving since then. Fifteen years ago the unemployment figures were the worst since the economic crisis of 1920's."

"And how much was that, Dad?" I asked.

"I think unemployment reached over 10% in 2009 or 2010. That means that one out of ten people wanting to work couldn't find a job," answered Dad.

Grandpa stopped playing with Hector, rested his back on the wall and said, "Actually it wasn't the worst since the economic crisis of the 1920's. There was a much recent one with higher unemployment."

"Are you sure? I remember many said it was the worst crisis since the Great Depression of the 1920's," said Dad.

"It was a hard economic crisis. I also remember those comments. However, it all depends on what it is you are comparing. In GDP terms, it was the worst crisis since World War II. In unemployment terms, the early 1980s crisis was worse than the 2007-09 one. During the 1980's, unemployment surpassed 11%," said Grandpa.

"Really? I didn't know that," said Dad.

"You were barely around in the early 1980's," said Grandma.

I interrupted their conversation.

"I don't know what that GDP is"

"Never mind for now, J.M." answered Grandpa. "GDP is a way to measure the size of the economy of a country. We'll talk about GDP later. Let's focus on jobs for now. As Obama himself acknowledged in many instances, putting

Americans back to work was priority number one for his Administration. For the unemployed, the slogan, *yes we can*, meant jobs were going to be created quickly."

"When something is your first priority you should achieve results better and faster than with other priorities in the list, right?" I said.

"I agree," said Grandpa. "I spent a little time this morning looking for data to help refresh my memory. I looked at the unemployment figures of other crisis. I took the 1980s recession we just mentioned for comparison as unemployment rates were the highest of the last 70 years. The numbers show the job recovery in the 1980s was quicker than the recovery during the Obama administration."

"Who was the President of the United States during that time?" asked Mom.

"Ronald Reagan," answered Grandpa.

"No way!" said Dad. "Are you sure President Reagan managed to create more jobs than Barack Obama? He was a Republican J.M. I thought he focused on other things. I never would have taken him for a social caretaker."

"Actually, Ronald Reagan focused heavily on job creation on his first term. When unemployment is so large, there is no difference which party is leading the country. Job creation is priority number one before anything else. Ronald Reagan was not a good economist at all, but he was good at selecting people that really knew how to do their jobs, and they did it."

"Still, it seems surprising. What comparison did you run, Grandpa?" said Dad.

"I looked at the speed in which unemployment decreased. Curiously enough, the peak unemployment on Reagan's Administration took place on his 12th month on the job. The peak unemployment also took place 12 months after Obama became President. With that similarity, I calculated how many months it took to go back to 7% unemployment," said Dad.

"And?" I asked.

"It took 22 months for the Reagan Administration to

reduce unemployment from 11.4% to 7%. It took 45 months for the Obama administration to go from a lower figure, 10.6%, to 7%."

"Twice as much!" I said.

"I've heard so much about the fact that the economic crisis during the Obama administration was so deep, and about the fact that Reagan was concentrated on international politics and star wars and so on that I could never have imagined President Reagan beating President Obama in job creation in such a way," said Dad.

My watch beeped. Dad stared at me, his eyes piercing mine. I guess he realized at that very moment I was recording the conversations with my watch. I looked away, confused. I knew he did not like me taping conversations of people without telling them first.

Grandpa did not realize what was happening. He had Hector sitting on his legs, trying to grab Grandpa's glasses. The beep signaled I was running out of memory space. I had to go to free some up in order to continue recording the conversation.

But Grandpa continued. "I ran other comparisons as well, and all show the same results. For example, it took 28 months to create 8 million net new jobs during the Reagan Administration, while it took 48 months to reach the 8 million during the Obama administration. And 8 million was a larger share of the working population during the 1980's than during the 2010s."

Dad was calculating some numbers with his phone, and added. "You are right. That's is why two years after the lowest unemployment rate of the 1980s, the number of net new jobs grew by 8.1% while it only grew 2,9% over the equivalent period of the Obama administration."

"J.M.," continued Dad. "Did you follow the discussion on unemployment?"

"Sure I did," I answered. "President Reagan was much quicker than President Obama, Obama took like twice the time. And I understand the lesson, as well. The fact that Obama was a Democrat and Reagan a Republican focused on space arms doesn't mean Reagan didn't care about creating jobs or that Obama did an excellent job at it."

"You are quite smart!" Grandma told me.

My watch beeped again. I needed to download its contents into my personal cloud but didn't want to tell! Alice saved me.

"Mom, is it time to go to bed? Was that your beep to send me upstairs?" asked Alice.

"Are you tired? You can stay for a little while, but if you are tired you can go and get ready for bed," said Mom.

"I'll wait Mom," said Alice.

"I have to go pee," I said, and got up to go upstairs.

But Mom stopped me. "What did you say J.M.?"

"OK, Mom. I need to go to the restroom. Grandpa, can you wait till I'm back?" I left the living room, up the stairs to my room, to download the info on my watch.

After I had emptied the watch's memory, I quickly went to the bathroom, then ran back downstairs, with the watch on recorder mode. That way, Dad wouldn't see me switching it on.

As I was getting to the living room I heard Mom saying, "It's certainly disappointing to learn that Obama took twice as much time as Reagan to get down to 7% unemployment."

"Mom!" I said, as I sat back on the couch, "I asked you to wait until I was back!"

"Don't worry, J.M.," said Grandpa. "We were just talking about the last data we reviewed with you."

He stood up and took Hector in his arms. "Anyway, what you just heard was not an oddity, it was just a disappointing fact. Many got disappointed because Obama's Administration couldn't activate the economy to create jobs at the speed they hoped for."

Grandpa gave Hector to Mom, took a minute to stretch his back, came to the couch and sat by Grandma, giving her a kiss on the cheek.

"So?" I said impatiently.

"As I said, this was just an introduction on the subject. The oddity is related with inequality reduction and creating better opportunities for the middle and lower working classes. If employment does not rise quickly enough, everyone would expect the Administration to use other means to improve economic conditions, to reduce poverty, and to create more opportunities for the middle and lower working classes."

"Aren't you forgetting something?" said Dad. "If the unemployment rate continued high for four or five years, wouldn't you expect the Government to increase unemployment benefits? I remember that being an issue of discussion, but I do not remember what happened."

"You are right. Taking steps to help the unemployed should be a high priority during an economic crisis. I also remember there was a lot of public debate on that topic. But I think there wasn't any new measures taken by the Obama administration during his first mandate."

Mom was taking Hector upstairs to bed, but turned around and said, "How come? What about his second term?"

"Grandma, could you look for news on unemployment benefits around 2014?" said Grandpa.

"2014?" asked Grandma. "Why?"

"According to the data we just reviewed, 2014 was more or less the time unemployment went under 7%. So that would be the time in which unemployment went back to normal."

Grandma slowly opened her foldable screen and asked for her glasses. I knew she was going to ask for them. She never remembers where they are! I found them on the kitchen counter. I brought them to her and went back to the couch.

After a few minutes switching on and typing on the foldable screen, Grandma showed something to Grandpa, then she projected it on the wall screen, a Wall Street Journal article[57]."

---

[57] Janet Hooku, "Jobless Aid Program Advances in the Senate," *The Wall Street Journal*, January 7, 2014.

The WSJ, January 7, 2014: 'Legislation to resurrect benefits for the long-term unemployed ...
The federal program of emergency unemployment benefits was enacted in 2008, during the recession, to supplement the 26 weeks of jobless benefits provided through most state unemployment insurance programs. The federal program allowed people to continue receiving benefits for as long as 73 additional weeks; that was reduced to 47 weeks in 2012.
After being extended 11 times, the program lapsed Dec. 28, [2013,] cutting off payments to some 1.3 million people.'

And the text.

MSNBC, April 26, 2014[58]: 'Listen, I [House Speaker John Boehner] made clear to the president last December that if he wanted us to consider an extension of emergency unemployment benefits, it would have to be paid for and it would have to include things that would help get our economy going.... They have not put forward anything with regard to how we would create more jobs. And so the ball's still in their court.'

"But as far as I remember, the fight between parties continued and nothing was really approved after 2014," said Grandpa.

"All this talk on unemployment benefits has been a bit confusing. What is the conclusion?" I asked.

Dad said, "The so called emergency unemployment benefits were created before the Obama administration, due to the economic crisis. The Obama administration together with Senate and Congress managed to extend those special benefits until 2012. On 2012, unemployment benefits were

---

[58] Suzy Khimm, "Boehner digs in against jobless bill", *MSNBC*, March 26, 2014.

reduced but remained over the pre-crisis ones. On December 2013, the program came to an end. Emergency unemployment benefits weren't extended beyond December 2013. But in terms of unemployment, the economic crisis had ended and everything went back to pre-crisis conditions"

"So there was no achievement out of the ordinary. Is that what you mean?" Said Grandma.

"That's right. So let's go back to the economic oddity and how to reduce inequality," said Grandpa.

"If I were Barack Obama, I would order to raise wages. That way all those with a job would improve their living standards," I said. I thought it was a good suggestion.

"It is not that easy for the Government to do that. You could somehow order to increase salaries of Federal Government employees. But the Government cannot dictate private companies or local governments to raise all workers' wages. You can increase minimum wages though."

"What is minimum wages?" I said.

"During the early 1900s, most industrialized countries issued laws requiring that any legal worker should be paid what was called *minimum wage*. A worker could earn more money than the minimum wage, but they could not be paid less than that amount." Explained Dad.

"And how much is it?" I asked Dad.

"In the U.S. it's around fifteen dollars nowadays."

"And what was the minimum wage during the Obama was President?" Asked Grandma.

"I guess that's what Grandpa is going to talk about, isn't it Grandpa?" Answered Dad.

"We are going to touch briefly on the minimum wage to move over to inequality," said Grandpa. "But before we start with that, let me go for a glass of water."

Alice quickly stood up saying, "I'll go". And she left towards the kitchen.

I also rose to my feet, followed Alice to the kitchen and continued to the laundry room. I opened the door. There was a thick smell, humid and sweet; the temperature was warm, but the dryer was not on. Laia looked up in my direction with a worried face. I told her, "Come on!" And she quickly crossed the hallway and ran towards the living room.

We used to leave Laia in the laundry room after her walk when she came back with her paws and hair wet from the rain. I guess she didn't understand why sometimes she had to wait in the laundry room while regularly she was allowed to go into the house directly.

I went back behind Laia. Alice was behind us with Grandpa's glass of water. I said.

"Grandpa, you were talking about the minimum wage."

"OK. I want to get into inequality really fast. But let's first analyze what happened with minimum wages. I can't remember what the minimum wage was at the time. Do you remember?" asked Grandpa to my Dad.

"I don't. But let me see," said Dad.

He looked into his phone and in a few seconds he continued.

"Here it is. In July 24, 2007, the minimum wage was increased to $5.85 an hour. J.M., you have to know that minimum wages are established by the hour. Then, in July 24, 2008 it was raised again to $6.55 an hour. Both increases had occurred before Obama became President. Then there was another one on July 24, 2009. This time the minimum wage increased to $7.25, or 10.68%. So, when Obama took office in January, 2009, the minimum wage was $6.55, and it was increased 6 months later."

"Oh, yes," said Grandpa. "Now I remember. Please, save that web-page where you are. We may need it later. Because if I am not wrong this info you just read would also be quite odd as well."

"OK. I hope you'll clarify the mystery," said Dad.

"I will in a minute," said Grandpa. Turning towards Grandma, he added, "Can you get us Obama's speeches on rising minimum wages?"

Grandma was onto something else. "What? Sorry, I was checking Barack Obama's Facebook. Did you know he has one open and live? What do you want me to check?"

I repeated Grandpa's request.

"Thanks, J.M.," she said and got back to her foldable screen on her lap. "I have something here from a page called *change.gov*. It seems to be a web page of President Obama and Vice President Biden. Yes, it's a web page in which they summarized some of their promises. This is what it says on the subject[59]."

The Office of the President-Elect. The Obama-Biden Plan, January 20, 2009: 'Make Work Pay for All Americans - Raise the Minimum Wage to $9.50 an Hour by 2011: Barack Obama and Joe Biden believe that people who work full-time should not live in poverty. Even though the minimum wage will rise to $7.25 an hour by 2009,
... As president, Obama will further raise the minimum wage to $9.50 an hour by 2011, index it to inflation and increase the Earned Income Tax Credit ...'

"Thanks. What-" was saying Grandpa when Grandma interrupted.

"Here you have a YouTube Video clip of Barack Obama's campaign on the subject. Do you want to watch it?"

"Yessss!" said Alice. I smiled. She didn't know we were talking serious stuff, not funny videos.

In less than a minute we were watching candidate Barack Obama in a speech at Monaca, Pennsylvania, literally saying[60]
,

---

[59] Change.gov, The Office of the President-elect. Agenda, Poverty, *'The Obama-Biden Plan'*, http://change.gov/agenda/poverty_agenda/ (published before the Presidential Inauguration of January 20, 2009).
[60] Barack Obama at Monaca, Pennsylvania, Beaver County Community College speech, *Campaign 2008 C-Span, YouTube*, http://www.youtube.com/watch?v=TG3BEjMm8Z8 (March 14, 2008).

'And I will not just raise the minimum wage every ten years, we are going to rise it every year.'

"There are a number of related clips in YouTube and other speech texts. It seems he committed to this again and again, all over the country."

"And I guess he didn't increase it every year. Is that it?" I asked.

"Worse than that!" said Grandpa. "He did not increase minimum wage any year during his first term, Obama started to suggest rises on-"

"Grandpa, you're wrong," I said. "Dad told us there was a rise on minimum wages in 2007, 2008 and 2009. Barack Obama was President by 2009."

"You're a bright, alert fellow, J.M.!" said Grandpa.

I felt proud and gave him a high-five.

"However, the 2009 increase wasn't an initiative of President Obama."

"You sure?" asked Dad going back to his phone and the internet page where he found the information five minutes ago.

"I'm pretty sure. You'll have the bill in the web page where you found the data," said Grandpa.

"I have it here. It was called Fair Minimum Wage Act of 2007 and it was approved with Democratic and Republican votes," said Dad.

"I remember it distinctly because President Bush signed this bill, though his Administration declared they didn't agree with it[61], which was awesome."

"Awesome! President Bush did not agree with rising wages, but he signed the bill to increase them. Then, President Obama promised to do it every year. But he didn't manage to get any increase. That's awesome Grandpa!" I said.

We went silent, I guess thinking on the irony of the facts

---

[61] Lori Montgomery, "Congress Approves Minimum Wage Hike," *The Washington Post*, May 25, 2007.

"How much did a President earn at the time?" I asked.

"I have no idea, but they had a salary, a house, white in color," said Grandpa, smiling on the implications, "expenses paid and so on"

"I have an approximation here," said Dad. "They earned 400.000 dollars a year. That is around 200 dollars an hour in 2011, or nearly 30 times minimum wages. When Presidents left the White House they were entitled to a salary of 200.000 dollars a year, even if they didn't work at all."

"Obama was earning 400.000 dollars and didn't manage to increase minimum wages at all?" I said. Today, I understand the kind of salaries that Presidents earn and the reasons to pay them allowances after they leave the White House. But at the time of this conversation I was really amazed by what I had just learned. However, I discovered more amazing things in the following half hour.

Mom was coming back from putting Hector to sleep. She asked. "Did you finish?"

"No, I said," jumping from my seat and walking towards her direction.

I joined her and shared what I just learned.

Mom was a bit surprised, and as she took a seat, she asked, "Are you sure minimum wages were not increased during the Obama administration?"

"We had not finished," Answered Grandpa. "They were not increased during his first term. I think he started to work on the issue during 2014. I remember because it was an election year."

Grandma interrupted and projected a text in the wall screen. "On 2012 there were plenty of complaints because it seemed like the Obama administration wasn't doing much on the matter[62]."

---

[62] Ralph Nader, "In the Absence of Federal Action, Some Voters Take Minimum Wage Issue into Their Own Hands", *The Huffington Post*, http://www.huffingtonpost.com/ralph-nader/minmum-wage-ballot-measures_b_2089641.html (June 7, 2012).

The Huffington Post, June 7, 2012: 'Since President Obama's campaign pledge in 2008 to raise the federal minimum wage to $9.50 by 2011, he has been remarkably silent on the issue during the past four years -- even in the 2012 campaign which has now come to a close. In the vacuum left by President Obama's lack of leadership on this issue, members of the 112th Congress proposed legislation ...

With a lack of initiative coming from the Democratic leadership in Congress and in the White House, however, none of these bills made it to a vote.'

"This article continues mentioning that it was local Governments that had to increase the minimum wage due to inaction of the Federal Government," said Grandma.

'In the absence of federal action on this issue, states and local communities across the country have decided not to wait anymore and are taking up proposals of their own to increase the minimum wage.'

Reading his phone, Dad said, "minimum wage history data by the U.S. Department of Labor confirms it[63].Amazing."

"However, there were some positive decisions taken by President Obama in 2014," said Grandma. And she sent another text to the wall screen. We read[64].

Barack Obama, Executive Order, February 12, 2014: 'Sec. 2. Establishing a minimum wage for Federal

---

[63] U.S. Department of Labor, Wage and Hour Division, *History of Federal Minimum Wage Rates Under the Fair Labor Standards Act,* http://www.dol.gov/whd/minwage/chart.htm (March 26, 2014).
[64] White House Office of the Press Secretary, *'Executive Order -- Minimum Wage for Contractors,'* http://www.whitehouse.gov/the-press-office/2014/02/12/executive-order-minimum-wage-contractors (February 12, 2014).

contractors and subcontractors. ... (i) $10.10 per hour beginning January 1, 2015; and .... (ii) beginning January 1, 2016, and annually thereafter, an amount determined by the Secretary of Labor'

"Oh! I thought it was going to be good news. In this Executive Order, the White House increased the minimum wage for contractors only. Not even for federal employees!" said Mom.

"That's right," said Grandpa. "It wasn't till the sixth year of the Obama administration that he took the first steps to fulfill the minimum wage promises. At that point, Republicans opposed fiercely, which gave President Obama a great excuse to say he would have done it, but it was not his fault he couldn't. He used his powers in a very timid way, as if just for show, instead of pushing for a positive resolution."

Alice stretched her arms while yawning. "This is boring," she said. "I want to go to bed and read a story with Grandma."

"Go brush your teeth and put on your pajamas, and I'll be right upstairs with you," said Grandma.

Alice stood up and approached Dad. She hugged him and laid her head on his shoulder. Her little hands around Dad's neck, stroking his long hair.

"Good night Dad," she said giving him a kiss.

She walked around and kissed Mom and Grandpa as well, and told Grandma with a warm smile, "I'll kiss you when you tuck me in."

And she left with a joyful skip towards her room

"Grandpa, Alice gets bored because she is a child. But I'm not," I said. "You were going to talk about equals and unequal, or something like that."

"It's about equality and inequality, J.M. It refers to whether people have similar or very different salaries, homes, education and job opportunities" said Dad.

"You mean, inequality is about rich and poor people and how much richer are the rich ones? Like the comparison you mention between the President's salary and the minimum wage?" I asked.

"Yes, that's it," answered Grandpa.

I had to show I was not like Alice; I wanted them to understand I knew what we were talking about, so I said, "I can tell you inequality is everywhere. I mean; the people cleaning the school earn much less than the school principal. It is pretty obvious. They have different cars too!"

"Speaking of inequality, there are two principles shared by mostly everyone. One is that all citizens should have the same opportunities no matter their races or economic origins. The second one is that depending on what is it that you do, you would have different remuneration," said Dad. "Having equal opportunities for all, regardless of social class or circumstances of birth and being able to prosper according to abilities and hard work is called the American Dream"

"The American Dream seems fair enough to me." I said.

"There are two other principles that are a bit more controversial than the previous two. The first one being that there will always be some people without access to equal opportunities and minimum incomes. Some disabled people are an example. According to this principle, the country should develop measures to avoid them becoming poorer. The discussion among politicians is to whom should the Administration aid and with how much. The second principle is that a modern economy shouldn't have too much of a difference between those with large incomes and those with low incomes in order to prosper. If the difference is too large, the economy is more fragile and, thus, more prone to economic crisis."

"The discussion in this case is how much is too much of a difference, right?" I said.

"Indeed," said Dad.

"Now here we come to the most important reasoning of our conversation tonight," said Grandpa. "If unemployment was high for a long time and unemployment benefits didn't increase, wouldn't you expect a Democratic President would take enough measures to at least reduce inequality and increase opportunities?"

"But what could he do? I thought minimum wages, employment generation and unemployment benefits are the means to achieve that objective," I said.

"Governments have many more tools at their disposal," said Dad. "There are broad tools like tax and fiscal policies. There are other policies targeted for low incomes, like subsidies. And of course, other initiatives more in the area of public investments that build the U.S. capital and generate employment. Improving the health of the U.S. economy is also key. These are probably the most relevant ones."

"So, did Obama apply any of these things Daddy suggests?"

Grandma answered. "He told during the 2007-08 presidential campaign that his Administration would take any necessary measures to reduce inequality and poverty. I'm sure Grandma has some quotes on it, do you Grandma?"

"Sure, here you have some. He gave the initiatives a powerful tag: *war on poverty.*" We read at the wall screen[65].

Gregory Kane, July 21, 2017: 'Here, on the other side of the [Potomac] ... every other child in Anacostia lives below the poverty line,". ... How can a country like this allow it?

Obama answered his repeat of Kennedy's question of 40 years ago the way Kennedy would have: "We can't," the senator said to cheers from the crowd. Then he outlined the details of how an Obama administration would fight its own war on poverty.'

"War on Poverty, that is the same as one of the Lyndon Johnson's projects, isn't it?"

"Oh yes. That's right, it was Lyndon Johnson's main initiative when he got to be President. Anyway, the same article contains other relevant Barack Obama sentences."

---

[65] Gregory Kane, "Obama invokes spirit of MLK, RFK", *The Baltimore Sun*, July 21, 2007.

'We can make excuses for it or we can fight about it or we can ignore poverty altogether, but as long as it's here it will always be a betrayal of the ideals we hold as Americans. It's not who we are.

In this country — of all countries — no child's destiny should be determined before he takes his first step.'

We heard Alice calling from the stairs.

"Grandma! I'm ready! I need to be tucked in, and you promised to read me a story."

Grandma passed her foldable screen to Grandpa, took out her glasses, put them next to the lamp on the side table and went upstairs.

"I'm going upstairs to Alice. You have a couple more quotes selected on the search tool," said Grandma.

She finished her green tea and left the room.

"Hmmm, you'll have to help me J.M. I am not as good as Grandma with this gadget, you know," said Grandpa. "This quote. Here! It looks interesting. How do you put it on the wall screen?"

I took Grandma's foldable screen and touched the upper corner. I liked this screen much more than my tablet.

Democratic National Power, August, 2008[66]: 'In August 2008, the Democratic Party released its policy platform and echoed Barack Obama's commitment to reduce poverty in America. The platform stated that by "Working together, we can cut poverty in half within ten years." The Democrats continued by declaring that "the fight against poverty must be a national priority.'

"And on the same web of the Democratic platform, Obama insisted," and Grandpa read aloud from the wall

---

[66] Democratic National Platform, "Renewing America's Promise" (pdf), page 15 - 16,
http://www.spotlightonpoverty.org/obama_overview.aspx#sthash.uTAg0w3D.dpuf (August 2008).

screen[67]."

> 'Perhaps most importantly, my plan will only focus on strengthening and expanding the most-effective methods for reducing poverty
> ...If my administration finds that one of its anti-poverty programs is not working, that program will be eliminated and funds will be routed to more effective uses.'

"Thanks J.M., could you put this other one, please?" asked Grandpa and I did. The following text appeared on the wall screen.

> Barack Obama, May 14, 2008[68]: 'A few days ago, John announced that he'll be running a new campaign, a campaign to cut poverty in half over the next 10 years. Well today, as John indicated, I want to make sure that everybody knows that he will have a partner in that effort, because that is a goal that I will set as president of the United States of America.
> We can do this. We can do this.'

I stood up and said with a presidential intonation. "*We can cut poverty, we can do this.* Barack Obama is using the slogan you mentioned this morning Grandpa, isn't he?"

"Yeah, that's right. What do you get from all this?

"Obama wanted to reduce poverty and made very specific promises on the subject. But, Grandpa, here you have a couple of other quotes selected by Grandma." I was happy to play with her screen. I projected the following[69].

---

[67] Spotlight on Poverty and Opportunity, "Senator Barack Obama's Written Responses,"
http://www.spotlightonpoverty.org/obama_overview.aspx
[68] Barack Obama, Speech: Grand Rapids, Michigan,
http://www.spotlightonpoverty.org/obama_overview.aspx#sthash.8O w0VYDC.dpuf (May 14, 2008).

The Office of the President-Elect. January 20, 2009: *'Barack Obama has been a lifelong advocate for the poor....*

... As president, he will use his life experiences to fight poverty and improve opportunities for poor families all across America. Barack Obama and Joe Biden will lead a new federal approach to America's high-poverty areas, an approach that facilitates the economic integration of families and communities with efforts to support the current low-income residents of those areas.'

Financial Times, December 4, 2013[70]: *'President Barack Obama called increasing inequality the "defining issue of our time" and said the decades-long trend was undermining economic growth and social and political cohesion in the U.S.'*

Associated Press, December 4, 2013[71]: *'Amid public doubts over his stewardship of the economy, President Barack Obama is putting a renewed focus on the income gap between rich and poor as he pushes for short-term congressional action and begins setting the domestic agenda for the remainder of his presidency.'*

"The defining issue of our time. That's a hell of a sentence," I said.

"So he set up an agenda to improve poverty and inequality on his first presidency, and continued

---

[69] Change.gov, The Office of the President-elect. Agenda, Poverty, *'The Obama-Biden Plan'*, http://change.gov/agenda/poverty_agenda/ (published before the Presidential Inauguration of January 20, 2009).
[70] Richard McGregor and Neil Munshi, "Inequality is 'defining issue of our time', says Obama," *Financial Times,* December 4, 2013.
[71] "Obama to talk income gap in Anacostia," *The Associated Press,* http://www.wjla.com/articles/2013/12/obama-to-talk-income-gap-in-anacostia-97632.html (December 4, 2013).

implementing more measures on his second term. That confirms it was a priority for him. Are you getting to the oddity, Dad?" said Mom.

"The right comment and question at the right time!" said Grandpa. "The odd thing is that instead of reducing inequality or poverty, both increased during the Obama administration. Income improved only for the wealthy while decreased heavily for the poor during his Administration. Poor became poorer, and inequality got worse than ever going back to the 1920s."

"No way!" I said. "I mean, how come? With all those commitments he should have achieved something, even if only for show."

Grandpa took the foldable screen back, and while he played with it, he said.

"Let's see if we can find some data on how inequality and poverty evolved."

After a few seconds of moving his fingers, he was still humming. He was much slower than Grandma.

I saw a section and mingled my fingers around his to post it to the wall screen. "Grandpa, here it says that rich people suffered more than the poor. That should mean inequality went down, right?" Then we all read.

"Good reasoning! During the recession, the rich were hit harder than the poor and, as a consequence, inequality went down momentarily. But it says it was during the recession years, that's from 2007 to 2009. We should find the data from the time Obama became President in 2009 and onwards."

Dad was on his phone looking for numbers, but I touched Grandma's screen and projected a new section. "Look at this. It's published in the same document at the end of 2013[72]."

The Associated Press, December 4, 2013[73]: 'The Great Recession of 2007-2009 saw the richest being hardest

---

[72] "Obama to talk income gap in Anacostia."
[73] "Obama to talk income gap in Anacostia."

*hit with 36 percent of income loss, while incomes for the
remaining 99 percent of the population it only
diminished by 11 percent.'*

*'The wealthiest 1 percent was, however, quick to recover,
capturing 95 percent of the income gains in the first two
post-recession years. The 2012 data suggests the bottom
99 percent of the population has hardly seen any
recovery so far.'*

"Awesome! During Obama's first term, the rich went
back to their preceding level of incomes, and poor got
nothing! You are right Grandpa. This is weird, especially
after so many promises."

"But there is other surprising data as well. Look at this."
And he touched in the right corner of the screen and
managed to post on the wall screen the following[74].

*Pew Research Center, January 7, 2014: '5 facts about
economic inequality*

*… By one measure, U.S. income inequality is the
highest it's been since 1928. …, according to Saez'
preliminary estimates for 2012, the top 1% received
22.5% of pretax income, while the bottom 90%'s share
had fallen to 49.6%.'*

"But maybe it was not so easy to get out of recession
and, at the same time, improve the situation for the lower
income people," said Mom.

"Actually, in previous recessions, Democrat and
Republican Presidents have managed to improve the
economy and the income of the poor in parallel. I had the
same idea as you, but I've seen a couple of articles on that
matter that changed my point of view" said Dad. "Here you
have it J.M." And he sent the references to Grandma's

---

[74] Drew Desilver, "5 facts about economic inequality", *Pew Research
Center,* http://www.pewresearch.org/fact-tank/2014/01/07/5-facts-
about-economic-inequality/ (January 7, 2014).

screen.

When they popped up, Grandpa said with a smile," That's like magic. You move the info from one gadget to the next, in a twinkle, just like that" -snapping his fingers- "I remember some phone manufacturers had an application to share pictures wirelessly between phones. But I never used it. I always sent them through mail or instant messaging. ...There was also this application called WhatsApp that was useful. But it was nothing compared with what you do now!" And he passed me the foldable screen.

"Come on Grandpa! That was when I was born. Never mind."

I projected the text Dad had sent. Dad could have done it from his phone, but I guess he knew I was enjoying having the opportunity to play with Grandma's screen.

The Associated Press December 4, 2013[75]: *'The study shows measures taken by the U.S. government to get the country out of the Great Depression efficiently contributed to curbing the growth of inequality.'*

"It wasn't only during the Great Depression of the 1920s. There has been recession and post-recession U.S. Governments that have improved living standard for the poor, unlike the Obama administration. Look at the next article. It compares the 1980's crisis Grandpa mentioned when talking about unemployment, with the 2007-09 economic crisis," said Dad, as the next text was already on the screen.

Ralph R. Reiland, Sept. 15, 2013[76]: *'The poor: Reagan vs. Obama.*

---

75 By The Associated Press, *Publishea by ABC*, http://www.wjla.com/articles/2013/12/obama-to-talk-income-gap-in-anacostia-97632.html (December 4, 2013).
76 Ralph R. Reiland, "The poor: Reagan vs. Obama", *Pittsburgh Tribune-Review*, Sept. 15, 2013.

I think the poor need another Reagan in the White House. The income of black heads-of-households dropped by 10.9 percent from June 2009 to June 2013. This decline in black income is more than double the overall 4.4 percent drop nationally in real, adjusted for inflation, median household income during the same four years of alleged "recovery."

Similarly, real incomes of those under age 25 fell by 9.6 percent over the same period...

In dollar terms, the median income per year (including cash government benefits such as earned income tax credits, disability payments and unemployment insurance) in female-headed households and black households has dropped, respectively, by $2,300 and over $4,000 since Obama's stimulus-led "recovery" began in June 2009.

... The Reagan years, 1981 to 1989, in contrast, saw real income increases and job gains for every income group, from the poorest quintile to the richest.'

"I don't understand all the gibberish," I said." But it is clear the rich did better with Obama and the poor did better with Reagan. This is also odd as you would say, Grandpa. You had said before that Reagan was a Republican. And Republicans are supposed to help the rich more than the poor. Or so I've heard Richard's father say".

"Wow," said Dad. "As I said before, I could never have imagined Obama did worse than Reagan!"

He then went back to his phone and continued.

"While you were talking, I made some analysis on the Census Bureau historical data."

Dad was capable of multitasking, being aware of several conversations at the same time and looking like he was doing something else. I always admired his capacity.

He used his phone a little more, looked at it and put a sarcastic grin. Then, he said.

"OK. Here I've got some additional weird data to complement Grandpa's oddity. Or I should say, the Obama Presidency odd facts."

After another pause, he said, "From 2008 to 2012, the top 20% households grew their income by 9.4%. At the same time, those in the bottom 20%, got their incomes reduced by 1.4%. Half of U.S. households didn't increase their income at all during those years."

Grandpa took his printed paper notes and said.

"Here are the Gini factors for income. J.M., Gini is an international index that measures inequality. The higher the Gini factor, the greater the inequality in that country. The income Gini index in the U.S. on the period of 2008-2012 went up from 0,466 to 0,477 or a 2.3% increase. So inequality increased while the poor reduced their incomes and the rich increased theirs."

"However, I remember President Obama was always talking about the recovery period. The question is the recovery period for whom. It seems it was only the recovery for those with high income" said Mom.

"From this I get two conclusions. One, that the alleged recovery shows income drops for the poor, African-Americans and young single women. Two, the fiscal measures of Reagan got their results and those that Obama didn't." Concluded Grandpa.

"But he sure did something for minorities such as the African-American and Latino, right?" I asked.

"Let's see the numbers," was Grandpa's answer.

Shuffling through his stack of pages, he found what he was looking for among his notes.

"If we focus on how poverty evolved, we'll be able to answer part of your question. Let's see, during 2008-2012, the number of white, not Hispanic poor increased by 10.1%. The number of poor among Hispanics increased by 19.3%. African-American poverty increased by 16.3%. So the so called recovery brought more poor people, especially among minorities."

"That is odd for an Administration that promised it was going to reduce poverty by half, and that got elected because of minority votes," said Dad.

"Grandpa," I said, "what do you think of this article? I searched for Obama and inequality, and I got it here, on Grandma's foldable screen."

Adjusting his glasses a bit, he skimmed the text and said, "That's a good article. Why don't you show it on the wall screen?"

When I did, he read aloud.

> *The Economist, September 21, 2013[77]: 'America's income inequality is growing again. Time to cut subsidies to the rich and invest in the young.*
>
> *Most of the growth is going to an extraordinarily small share of the population: 95% of the gains from the recovery have gone to the richest 1% of people, whose share of overall income is once again close to its highest level in a century. The most unequal country in the rich world is thus becoming even more so.'*

"But, Grandpa, if companies and banks raise salaries to rich people, inequality would grow. And you told us that the President can't change people's salaries."

"That's right. However, there are other means your Dad mentioned earlier, such as fiscal policy, which primarily is changing taxes. As a matter of fact, the article you selected mentions some actions the writer feels Obama should have taken, like reducing the favors for the wealthy." He moved his finger down and we read.[78]

> *'The attack on favors for the wealthy ought to start with the budget. America's tax code is riddled with distortions that favor the rich, from the loopholes benefiting private equity to the mortgage-interest*

---

[77] "Growing apart- America's income inequality is growing again. Time to cut subsidies to the rich and invest in the young," *The Economist*, September 21, 2013.

[78] *The Economist*, September 21, 2013.

deduction (an enormous subsidy for those who buy big houses). A simpler, flatter code with no exemptions would be more efficient and more progressive. A blast of deregulation would help, too. Many of America's most lucrative occupations are shielded by pointlessly restrictive rules (think doctors and lawyers).'

"Before the Obama administration," said Grandpa, "the U.S. fiscal policy favored especially those with high incomes. The Obama administration did some minor changes to the tax code. However, they ended having minor, cosmetic effects."

Grandpa stopped talking. Shuffled through his notes, left them in the coffee-table and laid back on the couch.

"You know, the tax code in the U.S. was complex and didn't favor the middle and working classes at all. It is really odd that Barack Obama didn't make a profound change in his first two years *in Office*. He had a Democratic majority at both the Senate and the House of Representatives. They would have been supported by some republicans as well."

Before he continued, he passed his hand over his baldhead in a very personal gesture of him. We knew he was thinking, so we waited.

He continued. "As a consequence of Obama's Administration inaction, or cosmetic actions if you wish, the U.S. became the most unequal country of the developed world, not in gross salaries, but after tax. After tax! The country wasn't that unequal when accounting for gross income. But by 2013, the U.S. was the most unequal country after taxes were applied. Can you imagine? Instead of having a progressive tax system, we ended up having the most regressive of the developed world under no other than Obama. Very weird! Read here, in the same article from The Economist." Scrolling down, Grandpa read.

[2013] 'America boasts the highest post-tax-and-transfer income inequality of any highly developed country in the world......'

Grandma was back after reading Alice her story.

Mom told Grandma, "Do you want some green tea?"

"Sure! I'll make it. Anyone else wants some?"

Mom and Dad asked for a mug with tea.

I said, "Can I have a Dr. Pepper?"

"Dr. Pepper? Are you sure, J.M.? It's a bit sweet before going to bed," said Mom.

I imitated this morning Grandpa's grin and said, "That's why. We need some sweet drink to swallow this bitter oddity Grandpa selected for today." And I laughed.

Grandpa laughed with me, and Dad just smiled.

Grandma said, "Oh, no! You two!" And she asked Mom whether she could bring me a glass of Dr. Pepper.

"OK, you can have one to sweeten the oddity as you say. But do not forget to brush your teeth afterwards."

Grandpa was waiting to go on. He said, "We are going to touch the last part of this oddity."

After a few seconds, he went on. "The fact that Obama didn't abide by his promises to reduce inequality and poverty were disappointing. But it was also very relevant because higher inequality reduces the chances of everyone having equal opportunities. J.M., the article you pinpointed a few minutes ago is a very thorough one." and we read it on the wall screen.

[2013] 'And a highly skewed distribution can lower growth, if it translates into less equality of opportunity for the next generation. This seems to be happening. The gap in test scores between rich and poor children is 30-40% wider than it was 25 years ago: given that the distribution of innate intelligence is unlikely to have shifted so much in a generation, that suggests that rich youngsters are benefiting more than ever from their economic and social advantages.'

"Remember that the Obama message we reviewed before, included a reference to *yes we can create equal opportunities for all*. During Obama's second term, people started to get worried about his handling of the economy."

"Can you imagine?"

"It didn't finish there. Your Dad mentioned two different group of levers to reduce inequality and generate opportunities for all: fiscal policy and a healthier economy. We just reviewed what happened, or didn't happen with fiscal policy. Obama's team insisted his Administration was committed to improving the economy too."

"How do you measure the economic development? I guess the unemployment index we talked about before is one way to measure it." I said.

"You're right. That is one way to measure it. Another one is GDP growth, which is how much a countries production is growing. But the crucial one to ensure the economy of the country gets back to normal is the country's debt, in this case the U.S. Debt."

"The U.S. Debt? What is that?"

"Good question! A country can ask for a loan as a person or a corporation does. When a family buys a house, usually they don't have enough money to pay for it, so they ask for a loan called a mortgage. Likewise, when the country needs to do a large investment, it usually does not have enough money, and it asks for a loan. Of course, for a country as for a family, the larger the loan, the greater the interest and the repayments. And if a country has large interests and repayment due every year, then it would have less money for expenses. So, countries as people, have to be careful not to increase their debt too much, or they will run out of money just by paying back the loan."

"So the U.S. asked for money to invest?"

"The U.S. asked for a lot of money before Obama. During the Bush administration, the U.S. asked for several trillion dollars."

"Several trillion dollars!"

"Barack Obama got as astonished as you. That's why he promised he was going to reverse the situation. ...Let me show it to you."

We were lucky Grandma was coming back with the tea mugs and my Dr. Pepper. That would make the search faster

"Grandma, please, come here. Help us find something about Barack Obama and his debt reduction program!" I told her. "I'll pass the tea around"

"Just a minute, J.M. Let me see."

She picked up her foldable screen from Grandpa's hands and started to look for the info.

"Is this what you are looking for?"

Obama, October 7, 2008[79]: 'When George Bush came into office, our debt -- national debt was around $5 trillion. It's now over $10 trillion. We've almost doubled it. ... But actually I'm cutting more than I'm spending so that it will be a net spending cut.'

Grandpa was trying to read on Grandma's foldable screen.

"What are you doing?" asked Grandma.

"Trying to read."

"You should have your glasses checked."

"Sure! One of these days. Now let me read!"

That was a typical answer from Grandpa. He did not like to go to the doctor. For him, it was like a waste of time.

Approaching his face to Grandma's gadget, he said, "Here. Can you put this text on the screen?" Then he continued. "After Barack Obama was in his office for a month and had reviewed the country's numbers, he was more precise and insisted on the relevance of cutting the deficit."

Barack Obama, February 23, 2009[80]: 'today I'm pledging to cut the deficit we inherited in half by the end of my first term in office. This will not be easy. It will require us to make difficult decisions and face challenges we've long neglected. But I refuse to leave our children

---

[79] Barack Obama, debate in Nashville, Oct. 7, 2008.
[80] "Remarks by the President and the Vice President at Opening of Fiscal Responsibility Summit", *The White House, Office of the Press Secretary*, February 23, 2009.

*with a debt that they cannot repay — and that means
taking responsibility right now, in this administration,
for getting our spending under control.'*

"The explanation was the right one. The implementation
wasn't. Obama inherited a Federal Administration with a
debt of 10 trillion dollars. By the end of his first year, the
Federal U.S. Debt grew to 11.9 trillion dollars. At the end of
the first term, debt had risen to 16.1 trillion dollars. At the
end of his presidency, the total debt had risen to around 20
trillion dollars[81]."

"That is awesome, Grandpa!" I said with a clear ironic
intonation. "President Obama implied that $5 trillion debt
increase by Bush was awful, especially for us the children.
He promised to reverse the trend and during his
Administration the debt increased by 10 trillion instead of 5
trillion dollars. So he left us his so called *'our children'* with
twice as much debt than the one he said we cannot repay.
Weird!"

"It took a lot of effort from the following Presidents to
stop increasing the debt," said Dad.

"Grandpa, this is very interesting, but it's running late,"
said Mom.

"We are just finishing. Actually, we could finish right
here. We could talk about other economic issues, but the
point that the handling of the economy was quite odd is
clear, I think. Is it clear for you, J.M.?"

"What would be your outcome from tonight's
conversation, J.M.?" asked Dad.

"The third oddity of The Obama Presidency, to use
Grandpa's words, would be that Obama promised the right
things for a Democrat: job creation, poverty reduction, less
inequality, minimum wage increases and improvement of the
country's economy, reducing U.S. Debt."

I looked to Grandpa to see his expression. He was

---

[81] The figures are as documented by the U.S. Government Spending.
2016 projections are based on consensus of projections based on 2013
figures.

observing how I gathered my thoughts to get into a conclusion, so I continued.

"I don't know whether he tried to achieve what he promised. But the weird thing is he managed to reduce unemployment twice as slow as Reagan, the Debt increased twice as much as the one he despised of Bush, and the rich got richer. The number of poor increased and it increased more among African-Americans and Hispanics, just the two groups that voted Obama in. Amazing!"

"Your summary is great J.M.!" said Grandpa. I could not have said it better myself. I hope tonight's conversation was interesting, though a bit long like Monday's one. I promise the one for tomorrow will be shorter."

"Yes, it was," said Grandma. "I agree with you calling this Obama economy odd. I mean, did he try to achieve what he promised, or he was just making promises for the sake of it? No matter what, Obama's economic achievements end up being weird!"

"Are the remaining two oddities as weird, Grandpa?"

"You'll tell me tomorrow and on Friday."

I got up from the couch, kissed everyone goodnight and went upstairs, yawning.

I felt a bit relieved by the sweetness of Dr. Pepper and Mom's words indicating the following President took care of the Debt.

Sleep came quickly that night.

5. OBAMACARE

Thursday, November 30, 2023 at 3:17 pm

The sky was cloudless, light blue. The sun was still high, and its glare filtered through the naked branches. The temperature was nice, just over 60 degrees, with no wind at all. The air smelled fresh and wet from Wednesday's rain. I was sure Grandma would be waiting to go for a walk. She loved these kind of days, and she loved to get out and walk.

The school bus stopped on our street corner, and we stepped out. I run towards home, practicing the crossover dribbling, extending the ball east and west that I learned from Dad. I was thinking about last Tuesday's special basketball event at school. I looked up and saw Grandma and Grandpa sitting in the front porch. Laia was laying by their feet. Hector playing on a blanket over the front lawn. Grandpa had a hat on. It was good that they were able to stay with us for a few days.

I continued dribbling and yelled, "Grandpa!" Then, I bounce passed him the ball; he caught it and passed it back to me. I kissed Grandma, gave Grandpa a high five and sat on the stairs with them.

"Why don't you grab a sandwich or something and we go around the block for a walk? We can take Laia," said Grandma. I knew it! She was waiting for a walk.

"OK! I'll pick up some snacks. Do you want any?" I asked as I went around the house, shot a three pointer, missed it, and went inside through the laundry room.

In a minute, I was back outside with snacks for everyone. Alice had left her backpack inside and was trailing my steps.

Alice took Grandma's hand, talking about the day at school, as they started to walk in front of us towards the little river park.

Grandpa took Hector over his shoulders and followed. I went by his side.

"I didn't see you this morning, Grandpa," I said.

"No, I got up after you left. I'm a retired guy, you know. That's one of the advantages. I don't have to use the alarm clock every day," he answered, with a sardonic smile.

"What are we going to talk about tonight? What is the oddity of the day?" I asked with a smile.

"Obamacare."

I tried to make a joke. "What's that? Was Obama ill during his presidency and taking care of him was an issue called Obamacare, or what?"

Grandpa laughed and said, 'Good Lord! No. But I'm sure you can give the word many ironic meanings." And he continued laughing.

After walking another fifty yards and still chuckling, Grandpa told me.

"Obamacare is the general name people gave to a fundamental health care reform. It was the defining project of the Obama administration. It took his Administration the full eight years of his presidency to implement it. By the way, its legal name was Patient Protection and Affordable Care Act (PPACA), also known as ACA."

"And I guess the oddity is that he failed miserably or, maybe, that he succeeded more than anyone expected, right?" I asked.

"Neither of them. It was very difficult to judge the level of success during those days. Half of the country thought the results were good enough, the other half judged it was a washout.... And probably, most of those opinions on whether it was a success or not, were based on feelings instead of on analysis. So their judgments weren't that valid, anyhow."

"Then, what's the oddity, Grandpa?"

He kept walking in deep thought. Then he told me.

"You know, the most perplexing fact was that there was a need for a profound healthcare reform. America was in a critical situation, a situation no other developed country was in as they had implemented the required remedies much earlier."

He stopped for a few seconds, and told me, "Let's do the following. Tonight we talk about Obamacare. I'll give you some facts. And then you tell me what the oddity is. Again, tonight's oddity is a very annoying one, but it has nothing to do with how successful Obamacare was in achieving Obama's objectives."

We were next to Grandma and Alice, and Grandma added. "Your Grandpa always had a very distinctive way of looking at Obamacare."

"Grandpa, please–"

But Grandpa had started to sing a song. "... If you have anything to tell me, it had better be tonight …"

"What's that song, Grandpa?" Alice asked.

"That's a song composed for The Pink Panther film. … The reference to the Pink Panther is my last comment on tonight's conversation. Let's go run to the riverside."

Alice and I stood where we were, with an amusing expression crossing our faces.

"What does the Pink Panther have to do with Obamacare?" I asked.

But Grandpa had already left.

Thursday, November 30, 2023 at 6:56 pm

I was getting out of the shower, when I heard Alice saying.

"Wow, Mom. You look so beautiful! I love your dress."

I wrapped on a towel and peered out. Alice was revolving around Mom, preaching her. She was beautiful indeed!

"Where are you going?" I asked.

Dad was leaving their bedroom, put his arm around Mom, kissed her and answered.

"We're going to enjoy our free night out. Grandma and Grandpa will take care of you."

They started to walk down the stairs. "JM, enjoy your conversation tonight," said Dad.

"Daddy, Grandpa said tonight is going to be the defining oddity. Are you coming back on time to take part in the conversation?"

"Nope! We are going to enjoy our time out. You'll tell me about that defining oddity over the weekend. Bye, bye, now." and he disappeared down the stairs.

"Mom," called Alice.

"What, sweetheart?"

"Can we order chicken tenders? And can we have dinner in the living room, in pajamas, like a pajama party?"

"Why not. I'll tell Grandma to call for some take out."

I finished drying myself, went to my bedroom and put on my pajama. I liked the Boston Bruins pajamas my aunt gave me for my tenth birthday.

Alice went downstairs telling Grandma that we were going to have dinner at the coffee table, in our pajamas, and she wanted cheese and chocolate with the chicken tenders and wanted Grandma in her pajamas, as well.

After a few minutes getting ready, I went downstairs.

"Grandma, where is Grandpa? We may talk about the oddity over dinner. He was a bit mysterious on this Obamacare thing."

"He went upstairs to pick up the notes and his laptop."

"Did Daddy tell you to call for a delivery of chicken tenders?" I asked.

"Sure, they are on their way! Do you want anything else? I'm cooking a bunch of homemade steak fries, -"

I interrupted her. "Grandma, make sure you cook enough fries. Grandpa always eats them all, and I want fries too."

She passed me a tray, smiling, and said. "Take this to the

living room would you?"

I did. In the living room, I arranged glasses, dishes and napkins on the table, took my old tablet and started to watch the best triples of the week.

Suddenly, I heard Alice roaring. I looked up and saw Grandpa seated on the floor, in front of the wall screen, with a laptop and the remote. I had not heard him coming. He was wearing bright yellow slippers with blue and red dragons, and a funny gold and red dressing gown -he said it was Chinese silk, delicate and stylish.

I giggled. Grandma was on the door with a face half upset, half broken, muttering, "He's hopeless."

"Don't you like my outfit? I like it."

"It's weird," I said

"I like it Grandpa, but the red and gold colors are for young women! And your slippers are for clowns" said Alice, chuckling.

The doorbell rang, and Grandpa started to get up. Grandma stopped him.

"You are not opening the door in that outfit," she told Grandpa. "JM, would you help me with the chicken tenders?"

When we reconvened in the living area with the food, Alice had helped Grandpa to connect the laptop to the wall screen, and they were on the couch. Grandma served the fries, and I offered Grandpa a cold beer. Laia came, sat on the other side of the coffee table and looked attentive.

Grandpa said, "You know? Red and gold are the emperor's color in China. You may laugh at my outfit, but it's a smart outfit in some parts of the world."

First the Pink Panther and now the Goldfish dress! "What are you up to, Grandpa?"

He took a bunch of fries in his mouth, chewed them, and said. "I dressed this way tonight for a reason. You'll understand the metaphor in the end."

We were finishing dinner when Grandpa said. "Anyway, why don't we start talking about the fourth oddity of The

Obama Presidency, Obamacare?"

"Grandpa worked the whole day to put together the info, JM," said Grandma.

"Well, it was so confusing at the time, that I felt the need to structure the logic. I did it when Obamacare was a hot issue back in 2014, and I realized how odd it all was and how misleading were some of the political discussions in those years."

"So what's Obamacare?" I asked.

"As I told you this afternoon, Obamacare was the main reform of the Obama administration. It was the flagship law of his two term presidency. The law was signed in 2010, took its first relevant implementation steps at the end of 2013 and the beginning of 2014, and it was still in the process to be implemented at the end of the Obama administration. The political battles around Obamacare became so frenzied and filled with misinformation, that most forgot about the problem the law was supposed to solve,-"

"OK, but what was the purpose of that conflictive reform?"

"That's a good question I forgot to start out with that, sorry. The Obamacare law was about the health care system. Though it may seem a small thing to you now, it was a very relevant issue at the time.... Alice, could you pass me the remaining fries, please?"

Alice took the dish with the fries and served Grandpa all its content. Grandma smiled looking in my direction.

"Thanks, Alice." Grandpa continued. "To understand the relevance of the problem, let's review first the status of the health care system when Obama ran for President."

Grandpa took a few fries. Then, he reviewed his notes, found the page he was looking for continued.

"In 2008, 14.6% of adults aged 18 and older didn't have access to any kind of health insurance. At that time, America was the only rich country without universal health care,-"

"What's universal health care?" I asked.

"Let me put it in generic terms. A universal health care system ensures that all citizens have access to healthcare protection. It doesn't have to include all kind of health care services, nor are the services totally free. But the idea is to provide a system that abides with one of the Human Rights. Let me see. I put it into the data this morning. Here it is. ... Great! You can read it on the wall screen! I'm a technology genius!"

"Grandpa," said Alice, with a grin. "I had to reconnect it all by myself,-"

"Alice is the technology genius!" said Grandpa. "Let's read from the Universal Declaration of Human Rights[82]."

> *Universal Declaration of Human Rights:* '*Everyone has the right to a standard of living adequate for the health and well-being of himself and of his family,... Motherhood and childhood are entitled to special care and assistance. All children, whether born in or out of wedlock, shall enjoy the same social protection.*'

"You mean the U.S. was the only rich country in which some of its citizens didn't have health care coverage?"

"The U.S. had several public programs, instead of an integrated universal one. There was private health insurance available, too. So, at the time, a large part of the population had private health insurance provided by their employers or paid by themselves. Most Americans aged 65 and older had access to health insurance through Medicare. People with low income had access to Medicaid health care. But these programs had different rules, loopholes and restrictions. The outcome was that a large chunk of the population was not covered with any private or public health care system."

"How many people make a large chunk?

"In 2008, there were around forty six million people without healthcare coverage."

"Forty six million! That's a large chunk!" I said.

"It certainly is a lot of people," said Grandpa.

"And what did they do if they got ill?"

---

[82] Universal Declaration of Human Rights, Full Text, Article 25, http://www.un.org/en/documents/udhr/index.shtml#a25

"When these people needed health services, they had to pay out from their pockets the full price of service and medicines. At the same time, others under the system, that was quite broken, had to pay a variable amount of the cost. In the end, over forty million people delayed medical treatment for serious medical issues due to lack of economic resources in 2008 alone." And we read on the screen.

Gallup, December 5, 2008[83]: The resulting picture is that 17% of households, overall, delayed treatment for a serious medical problem.

Among the 11% of Americans without health insurance, 61% tell Gallup they put off seeking medical treatment in the past year. This contrasts with 29% of those with private health insurance, and only 18% of those with Medicaid or Medicare coverage.

"However, in 2008, the health expenditure per person in the U.S. was the largest by far among developed countries."

Gallup, March 31, 2009[84]: 'Among the residents of all 30 Organization for Economic Co-operation and Development (OECD) countries Gallup surveyed between 2006 and 2008, Americans' satisfaction with their personal health falls near the group median despite having one of organization's highest GDPs per capita.

The United States, which spends by far the most among OECD members on health per capita ($6,714) and the most as a percentage of its GDP (more than 15%), has

---

[83] Lydia Saad, "Three in 10 Households Still Deferring Medical Care. Rate of deferring medical treatment has been stable for past four years," *Gallup*, December 5, 2008.
[84] Christopher Khoury and Ian T. Brown, "Among OECD Nations, U.S. Lags in Personal Health. Not feeling health benefits of high spending, *Gallup*, March 31, 2009.

only a relatively average Personal Health Index score (78) compared with other OECD countries.

"You mean that the U.S. spent much more money in healthcare than any other country and, at the same time there were forty million that didn't have health services on time because of lack of money?. That's amazing! That's an oddity for sure." I said.

After a few silent seconds, I added. "But that was before the Obama administration."

"That's right. That was in 2008. Most Americans recognized then that the health care system was broken and needed to be redesigned. They also thought that finding a viable solution was a responsibility of the government."

Grandpa clicked his mouse, and we read on the wall screen.

Excerpts from GALLUP Poll[85]:

'Do you think it is the responsibility of the federal government to make sure all Americans have healthcare coverage, or is that not the responsibility of the federal government?'

2007
Yes, government responsibility: 69%
No, not government responsibility: 28
No opinion: 3%

2008
Yes, government responsibility: 64%
No, not government responsibility: 33%
No opinion: 3%

"I see," I said. "We had a broken system, many people

---

[85] Healthcare System, *Gallup Poll,*
http://www.gallup.com/poll/4708/healthcare-system.aspx

without basic access to health care coverage and most thought it was the government's task to reform the system. So Obama decided to run for it, right?"

"Clever!" Said Grandpa.

"I could agree with him," I said. "I mean in a country so rich like America, no person should have problems to get treated because of lack of money or whatever."

"I think that most Americans would agree. But the controversy became so heated during the Obama administration, that most people forgot what was at stake. Anyhow, I've selected a couple of his quotes at the 2007-08 presidential campaign."

Grandpa scrolled down the document to the next page, and we read.

Barack Obama, June 23, 2007[86]: '*I have made a solemn pledge that I will sign a universal health care bill into law by the end of my first term as president that will cover every American and cut the cost of a typical family's premiums by up to $2,500 a year.*'

Barack Obama, August 28, 2008[87]: '*Now is the time to finally keep the promise of affordable, accessible health care for every single American.*'

Barack Obama, October 7, 2008[88]: '*If you've got a health care plan that you like, you can keep it. All I'm going to do is help you to lower the premiums on it. You'll still have choice of doctor. There's no mandate involved.*'

"So his objective was to make healthcare cheaper for all,"

[86] Barack Obama, Speech at Hartford, Connecticut, June 23, 2007.
[87] Barack Obama, "Democratic nomination acceptance speech", Democratic Convention, Denver, August 28, 2008.
88 Barack Obama, "John McCain and Barack Obama debate in Nashville," Second Presidential Debate, October 7, 2008.

I said.

"That's about right. As a matter of fact, making health care cheap for all the uninsured was a point fiercely debated among Democrats. Hillary Clinton was not in agreement with Barack Obama. In Obama's opinion those uninsured were uninsured because they didn't have enough money. Others in the Democratic Party thought there were people with economic means that didn't want to buy insurance."

"Obamacare was the most significant regulatory change of the U.S. healthcare system since the passage of Medicare and Medicaid in the 60's, wasn't it?" Asked Grandma.

"Yes, it was. And most people didn't really know what it was about. But let's move on."

Grandpa took his notes, found a particular page and continued. "President Barack Obama signed the Obamacare law, on March 23, 2010, after heated debate. I've prepared a succinct summary on what the Obamacare law was." And he read from his own text on the wall screen[89].

> *'Obamacare aim: change health care system and provide health care services to millions of Americans that didn't have it.*
>
> *Resources:*
>
> - *Change the rules of healthcare insurance to assure insurance policies include a minimum and do not discriminate, like if you have a precondition;*
> - *Subsidize private insurance for a range of people, under certain conditions (plans bought at internet marketplaces, called Health Care Exchanges);*
> - *Expand Medicaid program for the poor;*
> - *Oblige most business to offer health care insurance to their employees;*

---

[89] ACA law summary. Book author.

> • *Impose a penalty to anyone without minimum essential health care coverage and to any company not offering the prescribed insurance to their employees.'*

"Here is the first oddity, Grandpa!" I said. "Healthcare is a Human Right and the law fines people for not buying it! What kind of human right is that if it is an obligation?"

"That's quite a sharp remark, JM! I've never looked at it that way. But it's certainly odd. As far as I know, other rich countries have a universal system in which everyone is entitled to a healthcare system provided by their Administration. It is paid with taxes and special deductions on salaries. If they want a different service, they pay private insurance to get it. But you are right; I don't know of any country that fines its citizens for not having access to health care. As you said, to have some coverage is a right not an obligation."

"How much was the fine?" I asked.

"I don't have the numbers here."

Grandpa turned towards Grandma and said, "Grandma, I promised I would need little help from you tonight. But why don't you find information about Obamacare fines? I'd like to cover this odd fact JM has just discovered."

Grandma was tasting cheese with Alice, combining different cheese with different cakes in small bites. So Grandpa asked her again. She cleaned her hands and started to look around. "Where is my foldable screen?" She asked.

Alice and I got up and started to look around. Grandma looked into her handbag and in the kitchen. I went upstairs. From the front door, Alice yelled.

"I've found it, I've found it!"

I went downstairs while everyone was coming back to their seats, and Alice told me, "I've found it before you did! Grandma left it on the deck's chair when we left for a walk!"

"But I found her glasses." Was my answer.

Grandma put her glasses on, unfolded her screen, worked her way through the search engine and sent the following text[90] to the wall screen.

> *ObamaCareFacts:* '*Your tax penalty (shared responsibility fee) for not having insurance is paid on your federal income taxes at the end of the year. If your taxable income is below 133% of the federal poverty level, you are exempt from this tax.*
>
> *2014 = $95 per person per year or 1% of your Income.*
> *2015 = $325 per person per year or 2% of your Income.*
> *2016 = $695 per person per year or 2.5% of your Income.*
>
> *...The maximum penalty per family is capped at no more than 300% of the minimum penalty (e.g. $695 x 300% = $2,085).*'

"This is what I've found regarding individual penalties. There are also penalties for companies. ...But, wait!" Said Grandma. "There are some contradictory information. In this other article[91] the penalty caps are different. Both articles are from similar dates. Amazing."

And she changed the text on the wall screen.

> *The Wall Street Journal, March 8, 2014:* '*Roberton Williams, a TPC fellow, explained that the $95 applies only for relatively low-income households. For higher-income families, the penalty is 1% of income, minus certain adjustments, up to the average national cost for*

---

[90] Obamacare Facts Web site, Obamacare Individual Mandate, *How the Obamacare Penalty Works,* http://obamacarefacts.com/obamacare-individual-mandate.php.

[91] Sunday Journal, "Health-Care Penalty Will Surprise Many. Most Who Don't Buy Coverage Will Pay More Than the $95 Often Cited," *The Wall Street Journal,* March 8, 2014.

getting basic insurance coverage, known as "bronze"
coverage. That will cost about $3,600 per adult plus
$1,900 per child in 2014, Mr. Williams said.'

"Amazing, they didn't agree on the cap of the fine!" I
said

"That brings us to another amazing thing, part of
tonight's oddity. Confusion was all over the place." Said
Grandpa.

"For starters," he continued, "this morning I tried to
write a review of what was supposed to happen over the 11
year period of Obamacare's implementation. I checked a
number of government, journals and TV's websites.
Milestones weren't consistent across sources. Then, I tried
to extract the law milestones from the official document. It
is 1.000 pages long and so complex I couldn't identify the
main ones."

"It should be mandatory for laws to explain clearly when
and how they are going to be implemented," said Grandma.

"You mean there was information on what was supposed
to happen and when, but the information was different
depending where you looked? What kind of information is
that?" I said.

"Odd, isn't it?" Said Grandpa. He took a piece of cheese
and started to move his mouse and click keys on his laptop.
It was funny how Grandpa's moustache moved in synchrony
with his mouse.

Suddenly, the wall screen went black.

"What are you doing, Grandpa?" asked Alice.

"I want to change the screen to a different document I
wrote this morning."

"But you did just fine before."

"Yeah. I have a document here, but for whatever reason
the wall screen went black instead of showing my document
after Grandma's one."

Alice got up and went to Grandpa, moving her head
sideways and chuckling.

She took Grandpa's laptop and with a couple of mouse
clicks, she solved the problem. The wall screen was back

with the results of a poll.

Extract of Washington-ABC News Poll, September 2013[92]:
'Q: Do you feel that you personally do or do not have the information you need to understand what changes will occur as the new healthcare law takes effect?

Do have the information: 35%.
Do not have the information: 62%.
No opinion: 3%.

Answers by Party:
Democrats: 55% say they do not have the information.
Republicans: 68% say they do not have the information.
Independents: 66 % say they do not have the information.'

"Thanks Alice," said Grandpa. And to me, he said, "it's not just me who got confused. Back in September 2013, before the Healthcare Exchange registrations started, people felt they didn't have the information they needed."

"Moreover," he continued." Too many people were unaware of some of the benefits they had with the new law."

Grandpa scrolled down his document, and we read the next statistical result.

Kaiser Family Foundation Health Tracking Poll (Conducted March 11-17, 2014):
'Are you aware that this element is included in ACA?
Eliminate out-of-pocket costs for preventive services
    43% are aware it is included in ACA   .
Subsidy Assistance to individuals

---

[92] "September 2013 Washington Post-ABC News poll - Obama, Syria, the economy and health care," *The Washington Post*, September 19, 2013.

63% are aware it is included in ACA.
Guaranteed issue
54% are aware it is included in ACA.'

"Grandpa, you mean that no matter which party, most people didn't have the information they needed to take actions or to make up their minds about what to do? And some would get fined if they didn't do the right thing?"

"That's right. And others would lose their insurance by the beginning of 2014 without suspecting it would happen, as we'll see in a minute."

"But in part, people should be excused for not knowing, shouldn't they?" Said Grandma. "I mean, there were so many changes along the way, and as you just said, the available information was not consistent at all."

"That was a mismanagement of the Obama administration, wasn't it, Grandpa?" I said." I mean if this was Obama's star program he should have made sure everyone got the information right, at the right time. Why didn't he do it?"

"I agree with you. It was an odd mismanagement for a person that was supposed to be an excellent communications strategist and manager."

"But as your Grandma just said, it wasn't only lack of communication. The number of changes that happened along the way were also a factor in the miscommunications and another mismanagement oddity, if you wish."

"What do you mean by the number of changes?" I asked.

"When looking for data to prepare a summary of the most important changes in the law, I found that newspaper and TV's Internet sites are filled with titles like 'Another Day, Another Obamacare Exemption' or 'Health Insurance Deadlines Keep Slipping' or 'More Obamacare lies, no one is surprised' It was a long list!"

"That would be mostly Republican journalists, I would guess." I said.

"Most would guess like you. But, surprisingly, they were the same messages across the media, no matter which ideology. Of course, the language was more harsh and the news coverage more frequent in some media coverage's than others. But the message was the same all around"

"As I said, I've made a summary on what happened, and I took most of the news from what are usually thought to be the democratic based media[93], [94], including CBS, ABC, and NBC, CNN, The New York Times, The Washington Post, The Wall Street Journal and The Economist. I came up with this."

Clicking on the next page, the text on the wall screen changed.

'*November 2012*: *One day before the deadline for states to decide whether they would set up their own health insurance exchanges, the Administration pushed back the deadline for a month.*

July 2013: *Businesses with more than 50 full-time workers (Employer mandate) who don't offer health coverage will not be fined during 2014, as initially planned. Deadline delayed to 2015.*

November 2013: *Both, 2015 enrollment season and SHOP were delayed. The first one by a month. The second one by a year.*

December 2013: *Enrollment deadline extended three days before the deadline. Deadline was extended a second time, when that date arrived.*

January 2014: *Enrollment to high-risk pools extended for a month.*

February 2014: *Many companies (businesses with between 50 and 100 workers) won't have to offer affordable coverage to all full-time workers (Employer*

---

[93] "Admissions of Liberal Bias". *Media Research Center*, Retrieved November 26, 2007.

[94] Groseclose, Tim; Milyo, Jeffrey (2005) "A Measure of Media Bias," *The Quarterly Journal of Economics* (President and Fellows of Harvard College and the Massachusetts Institute of Technology) CXX (4): 1191–1237. Retrieved August 6, 2012.

mandate) until 2016. This was the second time the deadline had been extended.

March 2014: *Third monthly extension for the program known as PCIP, which was previously set to close Dec. 31, 2013.*

Final enrollment deadline extended. The Obamacare March 31 enrollment deadline extended (enrollment deadline for 2014).

Insurance companies allowed to sell plans that do not meet the standards, until 2016. This was the second delay of this requirement.'

"So, if people felt uninformed early on, imagine how pissed off they would be after all the changes. What a nightmare," I said.

"That was just half of the nightmare," said Grandpa to my increasing amazement. "The other half was all the misunderstandings created by the broken information systems and tools people had to use to gain coverage. Look at these quotes I picked up this morning about the issue."

<u>*ABC News, Dec 1, 2013*</u>[95]: *'Two months after the troubled launch of its signature health care initiative, the Obama administration on Sunday announced that its online insurance marketplace now functions smoothly for the "vast majority" of consumers seeking to shop for and enroll in coverage....*

A report released by the Department of Health and Human Services says the marketplace, which was down roughly 60 percent of the time in October, is now much more stable.'

---

[95] Devin Dwyer, "White House Declares Obamacare Website Fixed, But Problems Persist," *ABC News*,
http://abcnews.go.com/blogs/politics/2013/12/white-house-declares-obamacare-website-fixed-but-problems-persist/ (Dec 1, 2013).

The New York Times, February 13, 2014[96]: '*In view of the chaotic debut of the federal marketplace and many state exchanges, the White House urged insurers to give people more time, and many agreed to do so. But, insurers said, some people missed even the extended deadlines.*'

NBC News, March 5, 2014[97]: '*Federal officials have been steadily tweaking the law's requirements, making several extensions to deadlines, mostly because the Oct. 1 rollout of state and federal online marketplaces for buying insurance was such a mess.*'

The Wall Street Journal, March 31, 2014[98], '*The HealthCare.gov site for 36 states that have about 33 million uninsured people went down shortly after midnight Sunday and remained unusable until about 7:45 a.m. EDT Monday, a person familiar with the matter said. It was hit by a second problem around noon EDT that prevented new users from creating accounts, while some people who already had accounts were unable to log in, this person said.*'

I was really shocked by what I had just read. I looked for Grandma's reaction, and she was reading the quotes again.

---

[96] Robert Pear, "One-Fifth of New Enrollees Under Health Care Law Fail to Pay First Premium," *The New York Times*, February 13, 2014.

[97] Maggie Fox, "Feds Offer Two-Year Obamacare Delay for Some," *NBC News*, http://www.nbcnews.com/health/health-care/feds-offer-two-year-obamacare-delay-some-n45331 (March 5, 2014).

[97]http://www.nbcnews.com/health/health-care/feds-offer-two-year-obamacare-delay-some-n45331 (March 5, 2014).

[98] E. Ante and Louise Radnofsky, "Problems Likely Mean More Americans Will Enroll After Deadline," The Wall Street Journal, March 31, 2014.

Alice wanted Grandma's attention. She was playing with the cheese and asking Grandma to try some more cheese combinations with her.

"You look surprised," said Grandpa with a sad smile.

"I should have known better, but having both pieces of information in a couple of minutes has reminded me of all the suffering of so many people that spent days and nights trying to register, and they just got back error messages." said Grandma.

"That was what happened with the implementation of the parts of the law that got implemented." Said Grandpa.

"What do you mean," I asked.

"Some parts of the law were dismissed because the Administration discovered it was impossible to achieve them." Grandpa switched the text of the wall screen, and we read.

The Wall Street Journal, March 5, 2014[99]*: 'The administration said in October 2011 that it wouldn't implement a long-term-care insurance program that was a significant provision in the 2010 overhaul, in what was its first major policy reversal. The program, known as the Class Act, was shelved after the Department of Health and Human Services said its actuaries couldn't design a voluntary program that still met the requirements of the law that it remained fiscally solvent.'*

"I'd forgotten about this. I've have here a quote by the Chief Editor of the Wall Street Journal that had the same thesis than you about the confusion, Grandma."

The Wall Street Journal, March 6, 2014[100]*: 'Remember the original vision for the U.S. Affordable*

---

[99] Louise Radnofsky, "Plans That Don't Meet ACA Rules Could Stay in Place Through 2016," *The Wall Street Journal*, March 5, 2014.
[100] Gerard Baker, Editor in Chief, "Another Day, Another Obamacare

Care Act [Obamacare] when it was passed in 2010?
Congratulations. That might be difficult, considering the
delays and changes that have been made since it came
into effect.

Alice insisted in getting Grandma's attention, but Grandma told her that she needed a few minutes with us. Then she said. "I remember the Obamacare chaos of 2013 and 2014. It was always in the daily news. But because it was such a heated battle, I didn't realize what a management failure it was."

"Grandpa, your point is that Obama launched a health care reform that was needed. The effort was going to last two mandates. In the end, Obama didn't implement parts of the law, moved many deadlines, and changed other parts of the law and, as a final prize, he asked people to work with broken information systems. What the hell!" I said

"Isn't it odd that the most relevant reform of the Obama administration was a complete mismanagement? It is not only you and I. Any journalist following Obamacare had the same feeling. Some journalists and management consultants kept asking the question 'who is in charge?' but there was no answer."

The Economist, November 23, 2013[101]: 'The
Presidency-Emergency surgery Revelation after revelation
suggests that Obamacare's awful first month reflects
awful planning. McKinsey & Company, a consultancy,
warned health officials that the federal exchange lacked
"a single empowered decision-making authority". That is
consultant-speak for having no one in charge.'

Exemption," *The Wall Street Journal*, March 3, 2014.
[101] The presidency, "Emergency surgery. If Barack Obama cannot fix his health reform, his second term will be wretched," *The Economist*, November 23, 2013.

ABC News, Dec 1, 2013[102]: 'The new report also renews questions about the administration's management of the project and why many of the touted "fixes" weren't in place to begin with, including 24/7 "technical monitoring systems" and daily meetings about the site's progress.

The report also undermines the administration's early explanation that unexpected heavy volume to HealthCare.gov was largely responsible for the outages consumers faced. The culprit turns out to have been significant software and hardware glitches.'

"Others just concluded that Obama had approached a relevant, complex project too casually, saying it was the most catastrophic IT project in government."

And Grandpa scrolled further down.

The Wall Street Journal, January 8, 2014[103]: 'Given ObamaCare's complexity, a seasoned executive would have bird-dogged every stage of its creation and rollout, with obsessive attention to the testing of the sign-up computer programs, the public's first encounter with his signature initiative. There would be go/no-go inflection points and backup timetables, cold-eyed performance reviews and abrupt dismissals.'

The Economist, November 23, 2013[104]: 'The basic idea is sound: everyone must have insurance or pay a penalty.

---

[102] Devin Dwyer, "White House Declares Obamacare Website Fixed, But Problems Persist," *ABC News*, http://abcnews.go.com/blogs/politics/2013/12/white-house-declares-obamacare-website-fixed-but-problems-persist/ (December 1, 2013).
[103] Edward Kosner, Obama the Management Failure, *The Wall Street Journal*, January 8, 2014.
[104] Leaders Section, "The man who used to walk in water - An exchange you can believe in", *The Economist*, November 23, 2013.

The cash-strapped receive big subsidies, and insurers are barred from charging more to those who are already sick. A more modest version of this reform works quite well in Massachusetts. A man with little interest in details and a disdain for business, Mr. Obama tried to impose a gigantic change on the whole country all at once and far too casually....

The debacle of Obamacare has gravely weakened the president. In the days before October 1st, when the online health-insurance exchange opened, he [President Obama] seemed blithely unaware that anything was amiss. Using it would be "real simple", he told voters in Maryland on September 26th; it would work the "same way you shop for a TV on Amazon". Alas, it did not. Millions tried to log on; few succeeded. The website was never properly tested, it transpires. Although this was Mr. Obama's most important domestic reform, no one was really in charge. Crucial specifications were changed at the last moment. Contractors warned that the website was not ready, but the message never reached the Oval Office. Big government IT projects often go awry, but rarely as spectacularly as this.'

"There was an agreement among executives that Obama had little interest in taking care of details or in being involved in the management. He may have forgotten a basic rule: results happen when you work hard, not by desire or luck."

"Grandpa, how on the earth did Obama explain this nightmare? I mean; people would be asking."

"Obama used to blame it most on Republicans and their interest in derailing his presidency. However, the lack of management and the amount of changes had nothing to do, for the most part, with bipartisan fights. It was related to lack of readiness. And that is not something I say. It's something Americans realized on critical times. Look at this results from the previous poll of September, 2013."

Extract of Washington-ABC News Poll, September 2013[105]:
'Do you approve or disapprove of the way Obama is handling Implementation of the new health care law? (half sample)
  APPROVE 34%
  DISAPPROVE 55%

For each group I name, please tell me how prepared you think they are for the new health care law to take effect. The federal government?
  Fully prepared 10%
  Somewhat prepared 33%
  Somewhat unprepared 26%
  Entirely unprepared 27%
  No opinion 4%'

"That is amazing. Amazing indeed! Who goes unprepared to launch his flagship?" I said.

"It is odd that the Obama administration didn't communicate properly, didn't prepare for the launching and didn't manage the flagship as you call it. Odd indeed." said Grandpa.

I may have risen my voice because Alice and Laia raised their heads at the same time and opened their eyes, looking at me.

Their sharp movement attracted our attention. However, they went back to what they were doing. Laia dossed again. Alice continued brushing her index finger over the dishes and licking it with a happy face.

---

[105] "September 2013 Washington Post-ABC News poll - Obama, Syria, the economy and health care".

"Alice, there isn't more sauce on the dishes," said Grandma.

"Sure there is!" Answered Alice, smiling. "I'd put some." And she showed her greasy finger and licked it again.

But I guess she realized that she was being observed by the three of us and got uncomfortable. She decided to clean her finger with a napkin and tried a deceiving strategy, "Grandma, do you want more coke? Grandpa, do you want another beer? Daddy bought them for you."

"Sure," answered Grandma. "I'll go and help you."

"There is another curiosity, oddity if you wish. It has to do with who was profiting from the Obamacare initiative."

I said, "Whether it was well implemented, or it took time, in the end the uninsured got coverage and, therefore, they benefited from the reform. Those paying reduced premiums also benefited, I guess."

"Of course all those people benefited and companies in general were supposed to get some of the burden."

"What do you mean?"

"The healthcare sector, that is hospitals, insurance and drug companies would have more clients. However, Obamacare was supposed to reduce costs for people and government and be neutral to private companies. But the money flows and market values showed differently."

I guess my face was like a big question mark because Grandpa added.

"You do not have to understand it, but it means that investors bet that health care companies were going to give better results than the general group of companies. The Health sector was the most profitable sector in the stock market in the period[106]."

Grandpa went back to his laptop and added. "Let me see, here. This is a simple quote of one of the most prestigious economic broadcasters."

---

[106] Steven Russolillo, "Health-Care Stocks Lead From the Front. Sector Has Been a Top Performer in a Bull Market," *The Wall Street Journal*, March 30, 2014.

Bloomberg, March 12, 2014[107]: Investors are betting the law will withstand political challenges. An "Obamacare" portfolio of stocks that benefit from the law developed by the online broker Motif Investing is up 40.9 percent over a year ago as of March 12, almost doubling the performance of the Standard & Poor's 500 index, which returned 22.9 percent.

After Grandpa had red this last quote aloud, he raised his head, turned to me and said, "you look pensive, JM."

I was. I didn't understand anything about Standard and Poor's. But I knew that 40.9% was twice as much as 22.9%.

Grandma was back with Alice, bringing coke and a beer.

I asked. "If companies profited, people got cheaper insurance, and management of Obamacare was not the best, who paid the ticket? The government?"

"You are getting a Ph.D. in economy with Grandpa," Joked Grandma.

"That's a very keen analysis indeed!" said Grandpa. "And yes, it was the Administration, that is, the Americans with their taxes, who paid the bill. In fact, the Obamacare budget was estimated at... I forgot."

Grandpa took his notes again shuffled through them until he found a page entitled budget, and continued.

"The estimated cost of Obamacare for a ten year period, 2015 to 2024, was estimated at 1.8 Trillion dollars. But, as the same projections expected to get around 450 billion dollars in penalty payments and some new health related taxes, the total bill to be paid with tax money would be over 1.3 trillion dollars[108]."

"1.3 trillion dollars is a lot of money," I said. "I mean, we just review yesterday the economic oddity and all the problems repaying the loans. And the U.S. was already the

---

[107] Mike Dorning, "Americans Stick With Obamacare as Opposition Burns Bright," *Bloomberg*, March 12, 2014.
[108] Congressional Budget Office - CBO, Report, *Updatea Estimates oj the Effects oj the Insurance Coverage Provisions oj the Affordable Care Act*, http://www.cbo.gov/publication/45231 (April 14, 2014).

country with the largest health care expenses by far, with little results."

We remained silent after my remarks.

After a couple of minutes, Alice and Grandma realized we've become quiet, and stood silent, as well.

Then, Grandma asked, "What?"

Grandpa turned towards Grandma, and his laptop fell down from his legs. The wall screen went blank.

"That's a sign," said Grandma. "You two have talked eough. Time to change gears and help to put anything away!"

Dishes, glasses, bottles, napkins and pseudo-cleaned boxes were in disarray on the table. Alice finger had gone through most of the remaining chicken and sauce!

I took, the soda bottles and went to the kitchen to put them into the refrigerator. Grandma gave me a tray, and I went back to the living to pick up dishes and glasses.

Back in the kitchen with a tray filled, I saw Grandpa throwing bottles and cans into the recycling bins.

He asked me. "Are you tired JM? We could finish it here if you wish. I think we've covered some oddities around Obamacare."

"Do you have more things prepared, Grandpa?"

"I have a couple more things."

"Then, I want to hear about them."

Alice interjected in our conversation.

"JM you are becoming really boring, the whole week talking about grown up matters."

"I'm a grown up." I protested. "And you don't understand, but I do. Right, Grandpa? And it's going to help me a lot with my school project!"

And to Grandpa I said, "Could we go on?"

Grandpa took a seat smiling and opened his laptop. Then he told Alice. "Alice, could you help me again with the connections? It went black, and I don't know how to reconnect."

"OK Grandpa, I'll help you, but you have to promise you'll play with me tomorrow. No more boring stuff!"

"Tomorrow is the fifth oddity conversation." I protested again.

"Alice," said Grandpa, "We'll be finished tomorrow evening. I promised you we'll play the whole day on Saturday, or we'll look for something interesting to do together, OK?"

Alice hugged Grandpa and said. "Deal!"

She then took Grandpa's laptop and in a twitch the wall screen was on again, and we had a different text on it.

Grandma came back from the kitchen and told Alice it was time to go to bed. They left the living together, talking about the story Grandma was going to read her.

Back sitting again, I told Grandpa, "However, though 1.3 trillion was a lot of money, it was for a good reason. I mean, you said that there were more than 40 million people without health coverage.... That is three thousand dollars a year during ten years for each one of the 40 million people."

"Forty six million." Corrected Grandpa.

"Moreover! Cheaper per person. It is a lot of money, but if it served to get everyone covered, I guess it was worth it."

"That's a weird aspect of Obamacare. The law was large but had pitfalls. All in all, by the end of Obama administration, there were 30 million people without any kind of health coverage."

"No way!"

"It was one of the weird data that caught my attention then in 2014 and keeps me intrigued now ten years later. But I have checked the numbers with the Congressional Budget Office, the so called CBO. Its projections were used by the Obama adminitration as guidelines for some of their communications. So we can assume they were not playing numbers against him. They estimated that the number of uncovered non-elderly people at the end of 2016 was 30 million[109]."

Grandpa took a large gulp of fresh beer and said. "J.M.,

---

[109] Congressional Budget Office, *Insurance Coverage Provisions of the Affordable Care Act - CBO's April 2014 Baseline*, Table 2. Effects of the Affordable Care Act on Health Insurance Coverage, April 2014.

bear with me, because there are several other amazing numbers. Let's start with the number of people that Obama himself announced as having received health coverage thanks to Obamacare by mid-April, 2014."

He moved to the next page of his document.

The White House, April 17, 2014[110]: '8 million people signed up for private insurance in the Health Insurance Marketplace. For states that have Federally-Facilitated Marketplaces, 35 percent of those who signed up are under 35 years old and 28 percent are between 18 and 34 years old, virtually the same youth percentage that signed up in Massachusetts in their first year of health reform.

3 million young adults gained coverage thanks to the Affordable Care Act by being able to stay on their parents plan.

3 million more people were enrolled in Medicaid and CHIP as of February, compared to before the Marketplaces opened. Medicaid and CHIP enrollment continues year-round.'

Grandpa continued without waiting for my comments.

"In April of 2014, after the extended period of enrollment concluded, these were the numbers of people newly covered estimated by the White House. At the time, there were many discussion on whether they were right, or double counting, but I do not want to enter into that discussion. The thing is there were 46 million uncovered before the enrollment period. What happened with the other people not in the list on the screen?"

"And you have the answer, don't you, Grandpa?"

"As I said, there were many holes in the law. The one most fought about was that Obamacare assumed Medicaid

---

[110] The White House, Office of the Press Secretary, *FACT SHEET: Affordable Care Act by the Numbers*, April 17, 2014.

would be extended in all states. But as it wasn't mandatory, half the states didn't."

"Why?"

"It was a mixture of political positions and budgetary reasons. That is why most republican led states didn't expand Medicaid. As a consequence, there were people earning less than 11,700 dollars a year that weren't eligible for subsidies and didn't have access to Medicaid. Because the decision by those states was somehow political, the Obama administration blamed Republicans for the uncovered. Let me see. In the same source, the White House says how many were uninsured due to this very reason." And scrolling down, I read.

The White House, April 17, 2014[111]:
5.7 million people will be uninsured in 2016 because 24 States have not expanded Medicaid.

"5.7 million of the 30 million people is just a fifth. What happened with the other 24 uncovered million people?" I asked.

"That is an amazing thing no one talked about it then. But you know, the pitfalls in the law and many problems ended up generating this 30 million gap. Here are some examples of these kind of problems."

The Economist, February 15, 2014[112]. *'Obamacare. The law's delay. Rewriting health reform on the fly…*
In some instances, his tinkering may undermine his own goals. Amid public fury over the cancellation of some insurance plans, the health department in December announced that individuals whose old plans were

---

[111] The White House, Office of the Press Secretary, *FACT SHEET: Affordable Care Act by the Numbers"* April 17, 2014.

[112] 'Obamacare. The law's delay. Rewriting health reform on the fly," *The Economist*, February 15, 2014.

scrapped would, for one year, be exempt from Obamacare's mandate to have insurance or pay a fine.'

The Congressional Budget Office, February 4, 2014[113]:
'As a result of the ACA [Obamacare], between 6 million and 7 million fewer people will have employment-based insurance coverage each year from 2016 through 2024 than would be the case in the absence of the ACA [Obamacare].'

After a minute reading the wall screen, Grandpa said, "It was a combination of these and a hundred similar situations that ended up with the 30 million uncovered."

Grandpa continued. "At the time, everyone threw different numbers around. The influence of the economic crisis was also brought to the table. So in 2014 I decided to make a simpler, different analysis. I compared the percentage of people with health care coverage at the start of the economic crisis, 2008, with the percentage in the first quarter of 2014. The number was a surprise."

After a silence and a couple of mouse clicks, he pronounced. "Here you have what I consider the more striking numbers of Obamacare."

And we watched on the wall screen the following[114].

% of US Population over 18 covered by private or public programs:
Q1 2008: 85.4%
Q4 2012: 83.7%
Q3 2013: 82.0%
Q1 2014: 84.4%

"Is this right?" I asked. "The percentage in 2008 was larger than in 2014! Amazing!"

---

[113] The Congressional Budget Office, *CBO's February 2014 Baseline*, page 111, Feb. 4, 2014.
[114] Gallup - Health Well-Being Index. *Gallup. Polls* released in 2014.

"The percentage of covered people deteriorated with the crisis, as people lost their jobs and, with them, their company sponsored insurance plans. But in 2014, when employment was back to 6.5%, the percentage of covered people was still lower than at the start of the crisis. Amazing indeed."

"People are not dumb." I said. "They had to see what was happening."

"True. But many people became blind to real data when in the heat of a political battle. However, some of the media that had supported Obamacare, started to talk about dishonesty and lies by the Obama administration. Here you have a couple of examples."

The Washington Post, March 27, 2014[115]: *'More Obamacare lies, no one is surprised. At a House Ways and Means Committee hearing last week, Rep. Kevin Brady (R-TX) asked HHS Secretary Kathleen Sebelius if she was going to delay the open enrollment period for Obamacare beyond the already-extended deadline of March 31. She answered very plainly, "No sir." Rep. Brady didn't ask Sec. Sebelius because he didn't know the answer. The HHS has already delayed various deadlines multiple times. The question was asked to see if Sec. Sebelius would finally tell the truth. She did not. No one was surprised.*

...

Anyway, we're now at the point where the administration will lie to us, even though everyone knows they're lying and they know we know they're lying. I guess their strategy is to lie so much that

---

[115] Ed Rogers, "The Insiders: More Obamacare lies, no one is surprised," *The Insiders, The Washington Post*, http://www.washingtonpost.com/blogs/post-partisan/wp/2014/03/27/the-insiders-more-obamacare-lies-no-one-is-surprised/?hpid=z3 (March 27, 2014).

everyone just becomes numb to the deceit and the lies start to seem routine.'

The Economist, November 23rd 2013[116]: 'To make matters worse, this sorry saga has caused American voters to doubt Mr Obama's honesty. Time after time, when selling his reform, he told voters that if they liked their health insurance, they could "keep that insurance. Period. End of story." Policy wonks knew this was untrue. Mr Obama's number-crunchers quietly predicted that up to two-thirds of people with individual policies would be forced to change them, since the law would make many bare-bones plans illegal. But ordinary Americans took their president at his word; many were furious to learn last month that their old policies would be cancelled.
When Mr Obama ordered a strike against Osama bin Laden, he proved that he can be decisive; when he patiently built the case with China and Russia for imposing sanctions on Iran, he was persuasive.
So Mr Obama can get things done when he puts the effort in.'

"Amazing! They call the Administration dishonest."
"Some media did so, and so did the Americans that ended up disapproving the law at large, as you can see here."

Do you generally approve or disapprove of the 2010 Affordable Care Act, signed into law by President Obama that restructures the U.S. healthcare system? (March 2014)
Approve: 40%

---

[116] Leaders, "The man who used to walk in water. An exchange you can believe in," *The Economist*, November 23, 2013.

Disapprove: 55%
No opinion: 5%

"Americans also changed their minds on who should solve the health coverage problem. Remember the poll before. This is what happened overtime. Isn't it amazing?

<u>*GALLUP POLL:*</u>
Do you think it is the responsibility of the federal government to make sure all Americans have healthcare coverage, or is that not the responsibility of the federal government?

<u>*2007*</u>
Yes, government responsibility: 69%
No, not government responsibility: 28
No opinion: 3%
<u>*2008*</u>
Yes, government responsibility: 64%
No, not government responsibility: 33%
No opinion: 3%

<u>*2014*</u>
Yes, government responsibility: 42%
No, not government responsibility: 56%
No opinion: 2%

"And, in the end, it hit Obama's approval."

<u>*Business Insider, December 17, 2013*</u>[117]: *'President Barack Obama is ending his fifth year in office with the lowest approval ratings at this point in the presidency*

---

[117] Brett Logiurato, "Obama's Current Approval Rating Is The Ugliest Since Nixon," *Business Insider*, http://www.businessinsider.com/obama-approval-rating-polls-nixon-2013-12#!Ivc2w (December 17, 2013).

since President Richard Nixon, according to a new Washington Post/ABC poll released Tuesday.

Obama's approval rating in the poll stands at 43%. By comparison, President George W. Bush had a 47% approval rating at the end of the fifth year of his presidency. And all other Post-World War II presidents had approval ratings above 50% — with the exception of Nixon, who, amid the Watergate scandal, had a dreadful 29% approval rating.

The brutal numbers underscore what has been something of a lost year for the President. His approval ratings have been plunging recently as a result of the botched implementation of the Affordable Care Act. In the Washington Post/ABC poll, only 34% approve of how Obama is handling his signature health law's implementation.

"And J.M., remember, all this was to solve a real need that ended up not being solved." Emphasized Grandpa, while he moved on to the next article on the wall screen.

The Economist, November 23, 2013[118]: *'Perhaps the saddest thing about the Obamacare fiasco is that no rich-country health-care system is more in need of reform than America's. On November 21st the OECD published a report that highlighted America's staggering health-care costs and mediocre outcomes. Health spending accounts for nearly 18% of GDP, about twice the OECD average, even as 15% of Americans lack insurance. None of this will get easier as the nation ages. Obamacare tries to mend this, but it is a flawed*

---

[118] "The Presidency-Emergency surgery. Why is it needed," *The Economist*, November 23, 2013.

patch placed on a flawed system by a flawed president.
He does not have long to clean up the mess.'

"I think we've had just finished," said Grandpa.

After a minute, he addressed me.

"What would be your outcome of Obamacare oddity, JM?"

"I think the last sentence of the last quote has it all. If you launch your most important program, you should work hard at it" I answered. "And if you want to show results, you better be well prepared."

"Good. I found at the time that Obama's signature law ended up being such a mess, leaving 30 million people uncovered."

After a little while, Grandpa asked, "Do you remember the song this morning?"

"The Pink Panther one?"

"Yes, the Pink Panther's theme song."

"Are you going to tell me what the relation between the Pink Panther and Obamacare is?

"The Pink Panther is a comedy film series featuring an incompetent police detective, a French Inspector, a loser you would call him these days. The first film of the series was released in 1963, and its title was The Pink Panther.

"The Pink Panther was a treasured, large pink diamond. Pink diamonds are among the most precious ones. The diamond had a small flaw at its center. The flaw resembled a leaping pink panther, giving the diamond its name. Anyway, the film series is about the clumsy, inept inspector that is completely lost on what was happening."

I started to understand the sad analogy of Obama pursuing Obamacare, with all its flaws.

"But Grandpa, if it is so relevant for you, wouldn't you make it perfect! Flawless! Wouldn't Obama have made a flawless Obamacare law?"

"No way, he wouldn't," said Grandma, coming from nowhere. And with a sarcastic intonation, she added. "If the law and its implementation were flawless, they couldn't have so much fun fighting among each other! How would they all have fun if it works perfectly? How could they throw stones at one another? ..."

I laughed at the joke. And so did Grandma and Grandpa.

We were still laughing, and Grandpa mimicking the Pink Panther, when Mom and Dad arrived home, back from their dinner.

"Hi! You are enjoying the oddity a lot, aren't you? I could hear you were laughing from outside," said Dad.

I ran to the door and said, "It was a hell of an awesome oddity, Daddy"

"So, what is it about?"

"Before Obama, there was a large problem because many people didn't have health care coverage. I mean; it is unacceptable that a disabled person gets no care, or because one had an illness, he will not be accepted by the private insurance and not covered by any public institution."

"Right, and?" asked Dad.

"Obama proposed Obamacare. A potential pink diamond. Pink diamonds are very expensive." I explained. "So Obama proposed this pink diamond solution to all health care coverage problems. However, the diamond ended up with multiple flaws, and thus, it ended up being of much less value."

"Is that the oddity? A solution that does not solve the problem?"

"As Grandpa would say. That's odd, but it is not the oddity." I giggled. "The oddity is how on earth Barack Obama didn't manage to create a flawless diamond. Instead of having a diamond with multiple flaws and telling everyone it was a flawless one. The oddity is that he didn't manage the most important project of his presidency and that, in the end, the percentage of people covered by a private or public scheme in 2014 was not better than before the economic crisis."

"Good reasoning. I see you are deeply involved with this oddity." said Dad.

Mom was laughing. But not at me. She asked, "Dad, why

are you dressed that way?"

"This is the way the Chinese emperors used to dress. As an emperor, I don't care what you think about what I do. I know I am right, as any emperor should be. But if you want an explanation I may be so generous I'd make up one for you."

Grandpa started to laugh at Mom's surprised face.

Then, I realized the analogy and started to laugh with Grandpa.

Grandma, Dad and Mom looked at us in disbelieve

Mom told me, "time to go to bed!"

I went upstairs laughing with Grandpa. That is a good thing about looking at 2010's history from the 2020's perspective, we can laugh at it regardless of how heated the debate was.

6 TRANSPARENCY

Friday, December 1, 2023 at 7:33 am

It was a cold, snowy day, nothing like Thursday's good weather, as if the climate acknowledged December had just started.

On this snowy Friday, I learned about the storm that Mr. Snowden started in 2013 as well as its implications not only for the Obama administration, but also for any US citizen and corporation. That night of 2023, I made a pathetic pun using snow day and Mr. Snowden, though I didn't know the *'pun'* word then.

Alice was all set to go to school, waiting on the stairs, with her scarf, gloves and boots on, wishing we had 3 inches of snow.

I went downstairs, passed by and told her, "We aren't going to the North Pole, Alice!"

"Put on your coat, J.M.", shouted Mom from the den, "and don't forget your gloves!"

"Mom, Grandpa is taking us to school today. I don't need gloves, the car should be warm."

"J.M., do I have to explain myself again? Are we going to have the same fights every winter?"

Mom always wanted us to be warm, especially in winter. Grandma agreed with her.

"Women always feel cool and think we men have to use as many warm clothes as they think they need!" I mumbled in a low voice. But Mom did hear me. She always heard everything. I don't know how. It was like she had planted bugs, eavesdropping any word; no matter how soft we spoke.

"What did you say, J.M.?"

"Nothing Mom." And with a tired voice, I added. "I'm going upstairs to pick up the gloves."

"Hurry up. It'll take Grandpa at least 20 minutes to arrive at the school, and you don't want to be late," said Dad.

I went back downstairs and walked behind Grandpa and Alice to the garage. The car's heat had been turned on in advance, and the temperature inside was nice.

"See, I don't need the gloves." I told no one.

Alice sat in the car booster, and I took a seat behind Grandpa. Grandpa closed the doors, waited till we had our seatbelts on and pressed the remote to open the garage door. Slowly, we drove out from the garage and off onto the street. We turned right and continued down the street towards the road leading to the school.

"Grandpa, you didn't say anything about tonight's oddity. It's going to be the last one. Which one is it?" I said.

Alice blew noisily and said, "You again with this boring oddities thing!" Her face and attitude showed the scorn she felt.

I told her, "come on, Alice!" and to Grandpa, "Grandpa?"

Instead of answering my question, Grandpa asked me another one. "Do you know what transparency means?"

"Don't you want to talk about the fifth oddity? …What is this transparency question?"

"The transparency question, as you put it, key for what we are going to talk about tonight." He insisted with the question. "What does transparency mean to you?"

"I know," Said Alice. "The glass window is transparent."

I was sure Grandpa's question had a catch. But I couldn't get it, so I told him "You see, Alice knows."

"She's right. Transparency is the condition of being transparent; transparency is similar to clearness or clarity."

"So what?" I said

"Do you know that transparent and transparency could be used for people, organizations, speeches, and for people related attitudes?"

"Sometimes I hear that this or that person has transparent eyes." Was my answer.

Alice rolled up her eyes as if she knew better.

"That's a way to use it, yes. There's another meaning related to people's behavior. Let me give you an example. If the school Principal keeps parents, teachers and students informed about any school issue that affects them, he is transparent. He won't be considered transparent if, for example, he doesn't tell the relevant authorities that the school is short of money, and authorities discover it the very day it runs out of it."

"You mean, he is transparent when he is open to share, and he is not transparent when he doesn't warn others or he doesn't tell the truth, right?"

"Certainly! There is another example I want you to consider. Let's assume the school Principal tells your parents not to worry about your bad mosquito allergies during school time because the school will take care of you immediately and give you your first antihistaminic shot as soon as the symptoms surface. However, he doesn't know how he will be able to accomplish his promise because he knows the school nurse is leaving, and there is no one to substitute for her and no money to hire a new nurse. In this example, you could say there is no transparency in his behavior."

"But he probably really means he wants to take care of me, even if he doesn't know how to do it."

"True, he may have the best of intentions. However, if he's the boss and doesn't know how to implement those intentions, he's not being transparent with your parents as he's letting them believe the school has the means to attend a severe allergic reaction -like a school nurse- when he actually knows it isn't the case and won't be the case. And because you're allergic, it's a relevant matter."

"You mean, he doesn't lie, but actually he would be misleading my parents"

"That's it. A perfect way of putting it into words, J.M."

"That's cheating," said Alice. And she wasn't wrong.

"You are a smart girl, Alice!" said Grandpa.

I pressed on. "So you mean President Obama was not transparent?"

Alice asked. "Was he cheating?"

"Not exactly. But we'll talk about it tonight. And now, get ready. We've arrived."

The car slowed down and came to a stop in the parking lot.

"Bye-bye Grandpa." I opened the door and jumped out of the car.

Friday, December 1, 2023 at 19:19 pm

We had finished dinner a little earlier, and I was eager to learn about the last of the five oddities. So, as soon as I could, I went to the living room. Dad and Grandpa were already there. Grandma was sitting and Mom was bringing some tea.

I said, "Grandpa, I'm ready for the last oddity."

Alice arrived after me and said, "Grandpa, I'll help you in connecting your laptop."

"Thanks, Alice," said Grandpa.

"Have you gathered all the information and have you structured it as you did yesterday? Great," said Grandma.

"No way! I've been shopping the whole day with you. I barely had time to put together a couple of relevant data. We'll need your help here tonight."

Grandpa didn't like going shopping very much, and he liked to remind us whenever he spent the day at the mall.

"J.M., from our conversation this morning, you'd probably guessed that today's oddity is related to transparency." Said Grandpa.

I interrupted saying, "you were a bit obscure this morning. I mean your words lack transparency." And I laughed.

"Anyway," said Grandpa. "Let's start with some generic

facts. Most people have always sustained that Governments, including the U.S. Government, are not transparent enough. Among those criticizing the lack of transparency was Senator and presidential candidate Barack Obama."

"And transparency became another one of his promises, I guess," I said.

"Why do you assume so, J.M.?" Mom asked.

"He promised to change anything he criticized, implying no other candidate but him could do it. That's the meaning of the '*yes we can do it*' slogan." I said with a grin.

"You sound a bit sarcastic today, but I guess your observation is quite accurate." Said Dad, without taking his sight off his phone where he was playing another speed chess tournament. "However, it wasn't only Barack Obama. Most political candidates make a list of things to criticize and, then, they promise to change them."

"Indeed," Grandpa answered. "Nonetheless, J.M., you are also right. Barack Obama promised to boost government transparency. But he went further along, creating hope that this time it was for real."

"Why do you say that, what did he do differently?" Mom asked.

"Honoring his promise, as soon as he went into the White House as President, Obama gave a speech to all his senior team asking them to abide by his ethic and transparency promises. He also wrote and sent a '*Transparency and Open Government Memo*' to all Agencies under his command, with the same mandate," said Grandpa.

He took his laptop and continued. "I was able to retrieve the speech and memo after I dropped you at school and before taking Grandma shopping."

He was insisting on the shopping thing. I knew it wouldn't be the last time he insisted on the message.

With the laptop on his knees, he asked, "Alice, could you help me here? I want to send this to the wall screen."

Alice helped him, and Grandpa said, "This is from Obama's welcoming speech to the Senior Staff of the White House."

Barack Obama, January 21, 2009[119]: 'I will also hold myself as president to a new standard of openness .... Let me say it as simply as I can: Transparency and the rule of law will be the touchstones of this presidency.'

"And this is the *Open Government Memorandum* he signed and distributed throughout his Administration[120]."

The White House, January 21, 2009: 'Transparency and Open Government - Memorandum for the Heads of Executive Departments and Agencies

My Administration is committed to creating an unprecedented level of openness in Government. We will work together to ensure the public trust and establish a system of transparency, public participation, and collaboration.

Openness will strengthen our democracy and promote efficiency and effectiveness in Government.

Government should be transparent. Transparency promotes accountability and provides information for citizens about what their Government is doing.

Information maintained by the Federal Government is a national asset. My Administration will take appropriate action, consistent with law and policy, to disclose information rapidly in forms that the public can readily find and use. Executive departments and agencies should harness new technologies to put information about their operations and decisions online and readily available to the public.

---

[119] Remarks by the President in welcoming senior staff and Cabinet Secretaries to the White House, The White House, Office of the Press Secretary, January 21, 2009.

[120] The White House web page on 'Transparency and Open Government', under Barack Obama.

Executive departments and agencies should also solicit public feedback to identify information of greatest use to the public.

.....

BARACK OBAMA.'

"Wow! He was busy on his first working days. He signed so many documents and gave so many speeches. At least one per oddity!" Said Mom.

"Grandpa, you should have read us this text this morning when trying to define transparency. Obama was pretty clear!" I said.

"Crystal-clear." said Mom, smiling. And she added. "Most hoped he would increase the level of transparency and ethics."

Alice asked Grandma. "Can I work on your hair? I can make you a unique hairstyle."

"Sure, sweat heart. What kind of hairstyle are you going to make?"

"A queen's one. It's like a princess one, but for old people." And she ran upstairs to pick up her hair brushes.

I looked at Grandma as if she was a reckless woman, but said nothing and followed with our discussion

"And in a way, he did deliver some transparency. However, it was mostly in relation to what happened under other Administrations, not on his own one," said Grandpa.

Dad was interested and, though he continued focused on his speed chess game online, you could tell he was also listening to our discussion.

"What do you mean by that?"

"He ordered to disclose some classified records and to reduce the non-disclosure periods for records dated before 2009. The changes he did regarding his own Administration ended up being cosmetic most of the time, such as the disclosure about the White House list of visitors, though that was after nine months of asking him to abide by his promises of being transparent. You can see it in this two articles." He then sent the following text to the wall screen.

NBC News, June 16, 2009[121]: 'Obama bloks list of visitors to White House. Taking Bush position, Obama denies msnbc.com request.

The Obama administration is fighting to block access to names of visitors to the White House, taking up the Bush administration argument that a president doesn't have to reveal who comes calling to influence policy decisions.

Despite President Barack Obama's pledge to introduce a new era of transparency to Washington, and despite two rulings by a federal judge that the records are public, the Secret Service has denied msnbc.com's request for the names of all White House visitors from Jan. 20 to the present. It also denied a narrower request by the nonpartisan watchdog group Citizens for Responsibility and Ethics in Washington, which sought logs of visits by executives of coal companies.

Updated: CREW says it filed suit Tuesday against the Department of Homeland Security, which oversees the Secret Service. Here's a copy of CREW's complaint.

"We are deeply disappointed," said CREW attorney Anne L. Weismann, "that the Obama administration is following the same anti-transparency policy as the Bush administration when it comes to White House visitor records. Refusing to let the public know who visits the White House is not the action of a pro-transparency, pro-accountability administration."

---

[121] Bill Dedman, "Obama bloks list of visitors to White House. Taking Bush position, Obama denies msnbc.com request for logs," *NBC News*, http://www.nbcnews.com/id/31373407/ns/politics-white_house/t/obama-blocks-list-visitors-white-house/#.U25tzfl5OSo (updated June 16, 2009).

The New York Times, October 30, 2009[122]: *'The Obama administration on Friday released a partial roster of visitors in the first six months of President Obama's term, a disclosure that shows business executives, labor leaders, lobbyists and a sprinkling of celebrities were cleared into the White House for meetings, events or tours.*

... The White House released the names late Friday in a disclosure that officials said was without precedent by previous administrations. The names on the White House Web site were in response to requests about specific people by watchdog groups or news organizations. By December, the White House intends to regularly release names of visitors in three-month increments.'

"However, even in 2013, the White House was cherishing this as a significant transparency development of his Administration." And we read.

Politico, October 11, 2013[123]: *'In his statement to POLITICO, Schultz said the Obama administration had an "unparalleled commitment to reforming Washington."*

"As part of the President's unparalleled commitment to reforming Washington, this Administration is the first ever to release White House visitor records," Schultz said.'

"I noticed a bit of irony in your comment," said Dad.
"You noticed correctly. In the opinion of many

---

[122] Jeff Zeleny, "White House Visitor Log Lists Stars and C.E.O.'s," *The New York Times*, October 30, 2009.

[123] Dylan Byers, "White House defends transparency record after scathing CPJ report, *Politico*, http://www.politico.com/blogs/media/2013/10/white-house-defends-transparency-record-after-scathing-174867.html (October 11, 2013).

connoisseurs, the Obama administration didn't show openness, fairness and transparency in other more subtle or relevant issues."

"I think I remember, but could you give us any examples, Grandpa?" Dad asked.

"Sure! Lobbying is a perfect one." Grandpa answered.

Alice was back with brushes, rollers, a large comb and some other stuff. "Grandma, can you move to this chair please?"

Mom told her, "Alice, Grandma's going to be uncomfortable on that low chair."

"But her head is too high now."

"Don't worry, I'll move."

But before Grandma moved, Alice had disappeared, running towards the kitchen.

"J.M., do you know what a Lobbyist is?" Mom asked me.

"No, I don't really know. What is it?"

"A Lobbyist is a person or an organization whose job is to persuade members of Congress and Senate to vote in favor of a law. They also lobby the Administration for decisions like buying equipment following the specs favorable for this or that supplier, as an example." Explained Dad. "They're paid by those who would like the legislation to be approved or their products and services to be bought."

"I think I understand, but could you explain it a bit more Daddy?"

"Let's assume a company or institution would like certain rules to become or be included in the law because it would be good for their interests. This company or institution, along with other companies hire someone to go around explaining Congressmen the benefits of the law, and showing how good it is for their constituencies, so they'd give their positive vote to the law. That someone is called *Lobbyist*."

"So the one that has more money to pay lobbyist is the one that gets its law approved?"

Grandpa answered saying. "Actually, the lobby business is regulated in the U.S. in order to avoid misbehaviors. However, Candidate Obama agreed with many citizens that the lobbyist had too much influence. He made specific promises when campaigning... I had some quotes on my laptop. Here."

Barack Obama, June 22, 2007[124]: "When you walk into my administration, you will not be able to work on regulations or contracts directly related to your former employer for two years."

Barack Obama, November 10, 2007[125]: "I am in this race to tell the corporate lobbyists that their days of setting the agenda in Washington are over. I have done more than any other candidate in this race to take on lobbyists — and won. They have not funded my campaign, they will not run my White House, and they will not drown out the voices of the American people when I am president."

"He issued many equivalent remarks during his presidential campaign, and when he took Office, he signed an Executive Order -- *Ethics Commitments by Executive Branch Personnel*[126]. He announced it as the most sweeping ethics rules in American history, ones that would 'close the revolving door that lets lobbyists come into government freely'."

"This Executive Order, was in addition to the Memorandum we just read?" Dad asked.

"And did he close the *revolving door*?" I asked.

Grandpa answered, "Yes", and turning to me, he went on. "Just on the contrary. Shortly after taking Office, President Obama nominated William Lynn, a top executive of a defense company and a registered defense lobbyist, to be deputy defense secretary under his command."

---

[124] Barack Obama, Speech in Manchester, NH, June 22, 2007.
[125] Barack Obama, Speech in Des Moines, IA, November 10, 2007.
[126] Executive Order *13490-- Ethics Commitments by Executive Branch Personnel*, January 21, 2009.

"No kidding!" I said.

Alice was back with a stool. She jumped on it and started working on Grandma's hair.

"I retrieved some newspaper articles on the subject. You are not the first one to be surprised" said Grandpa, clicking a key with a wide smile of satisfaction. Technology was working just fine. We could read on the wall screen.

> _Time, Jan. 27, 2009_[127]: _'Last year the Pentagon paid the Raytheon Corp., its fifth largest contractor, a cool $10 billion for its missiles, missile shields and a constellation of electronics. This year President Barack Obama is putting Raytheon's recently departed top lobbyist in charge of the Pentagon's day-to-day management._
>
> _In Washington that almost qualifies as business as usual, except for a small detail: on the campaign trail, Obama vowed to stop the revolving door that lets onetime lobbyists go to work for the Federal Government and oversee contracts that could harm — or help — their former employer. And one of the first things the new President did in office was seemingly make good on that promise, signing an Executive Order barring former lobbyists from joining his Administration to work at agencies they recently lobbied._
>
> _Not surprisingly, Obama's good-government backers were less than pleased to see the President, only a few days after signing the blanket ban, issue a waiver permitting William Lynn to serve as Deputy Secretary of Defense.'_

"What kind of weird game was that?" I asked. "It certainly reminds me on what you told me earlier this

---

[127] Mark Thompson, "Obama's Lobbyist Ban Meets a Loophole: William Lynn," _Time_, January. 27, 2009.

morning about deciding and talking one thing but behaving in a different way."

Dad raised his eyes from his chess game and said, "Was it a well justified waiver?"

"Mr. William had a good resume for the position. However, many believed that President Obama should have delayed the signing of the ethics guidelines, or should have chosen another candidate. Even if he wasn't interested in living by the standards, the President should be more subtle. This behavior could be interpreted as a message that President Obama didn't care that much about his own ethics rules."

"Unfortunately, it took him less than a month to break the same rules again. On February 20, 2009, President Obama issued another two waivers to Lobbyists Jocelyn Frye and Cecilia Muñoz."

ABC News, March 10, 2009[128]: 'The White House Tuesday evening disclosed that almost three weeks ago the Obama administration granted ethics waivers for two additional officials who had previously worked as lobbyists. On February 20 the administration signed waivers for Jocelyn Frye, former general counsel at the National Partnership for Women & Families, and Cecilia Muñoz, the former senior vice president for the National Council of La Raza, allowing them to work on issues for which they lobbied.'

"Didn't President Obama promise that no Lobbyist would find a job in his Administration?" Asked Dad. "If that's the case I would agree with you. He should have looked for other candidates this time around."

"Yes he did promise. Barack Obama on his remarks at a Campaign Event in Spartanburg, SC, on November 3, 2007 said.

---

[128] Tahman Bradley, "Obama White House Discloses Two More Lobbyist Waivers Granted," *ABC News*, March 10, 2009.

Barack Obama, November 3, 2007:'I don't take a dime of their [lobbyist] money, and when I am President, they won't find a job in my White House.'

Grandpa looked into his computer and said, "But it wasn't just these three, he hired more than one hundred!"

"It was *his* White House, or so he said in the article Grandpa put a little while ago. So he did as he pleased with *his* own house. So he changed his mind and hired who he wanted." I said trying to make a joke. But they were taking the subject seriously, and no one laughed.

Then Grandpa clicked on a key and the wall screen went blank. "I don't understand, he said. I have it here on my screen."

Alice stepped down from the stool and left Grandma's hair with a funny shape. She asked Grandpa if she could help, but took the laptop from him without waiting for an answer.

While Alice was working on Grandpa's laptop, he said. "A well-known scholar, Conor McGrath, researched the problem. He found 119 former lobbyist worked at the Obama administration[129] and published it in a prestigious journal."

After a couple of keystrokes, we could read about it on the screen.

Washington Examiner, July 23, 2013[130]: "President Obama's public rhetoric on contact with lobbyists does not always accord with his private actions," lobbying scholar Conor McGrath writes in the latest issue of the Journal of Public Affairs.

---

[129] Conor McGrath, "'They are not my people': Barack Obama on lobbying and lobbyists," *Journal of Public Affairs*, Article first published online, June 25, 2013, DOI: 10.1002/pa.1481. Iin paper on Volume 13, issue 3 pages 308 to 328, August 2013.

[130] Timothy P. Carney, "Obama administration packed with lobbyists he vowed not to hire," *Washington Examiner*, July 23, 2013.

... you should read McGrath's paper - or at least study Table 1 and Table 2, which list the lobbyists who entered the Obama administration and the administration officials who have cashed out to K Street. McGrath's lobbyist count in the Obama administration is the most thorough count to date.

... Obama said in his 2010 State of the Union "we have excluded lobbyists from policymaking jobs." David Axelrod said in 2011 that Obama "has ended the revolving door between industry and government.... He doesn't, uh, hire lobbyists."

...

McGrath finds 119 former lobbyists in the Obama administration. The administration employs former in-house lobbyists from Microsoft, Fannie Mae, insurance giant Wellpoint, AT&T, Verizon, Sprint, Monsanto, Yahoo, Google, Microsoft, Raytheon, and Goldman Sachs. Obama has hired from the ranks of K Street firms Cassidy & Associates, Covington & Burling, Heather Podesta & Partners, Akin Gump, Arnold & Porter, Winston & Strawn, Timmons & Co., and others.

And that's only the incoming side of the revolving door. McGrath's Table 2 covers the more insidious direction: Those Obama officials who monetize their public service by becoming lobbyists. McGrath lists 37 Obama alumni now on K Street.'

"One hundred and nineteen former lobbyists on his first term alone!" Said Dad. "Obama wasn't as good a doorkeeper of the so called lobbyist revolving door."

We all went silent.

Alice broke the silence. "Grandma. Here, take the queen's mirror" -giggling- "What style do you prefer?"

She was holding Grandma's hair, and put it into different bun shapes. She had clipped some bright threads to Grandma's hair. I didn't understand, but Grandma did. She gave Alice some instructions.

While watching them trying hairstyles I thought about what I just heard. It wasn't enough to become one of Grandpa's five oddities. But I have learned from my experience on the days before how Grandpa was structuring these conversations. So I said.

"Though it seems quite an amazing behavior contrary to his own mandate, I'm sure it's not what defines the oddity of tonight, right?"

Grandpa smiled. "You're right, J.M. This is just one angle. Another one is when lack of transparency is used to convey an image that differs strongly with reality."

"You mean to lie."

"Not exactly, I mean to give a false impression, which is more subtle than lying. Let's think of an example," said Grandpa. "Do you remember last Monday when we talked about drone bombings?"

"Sure I do. President Obama approved more drone bombings in his first year as President than Bush in his entire presidency or something like that. I remember that the year Barack Obama accepted the Nobel Peace Prize, the U.S. sent one or two drone bombs every week into countries that were not at war."

"You've got a great memory. At that time, there was a lack of communication on what was the Obama administration doing. When asked, officials answered the bombings were sporadic, targeted and needed."

"Who defined one or two bombings a week as sporadically?" I asked.

"What I mean is that the lack of information along with the specific word dropping, like *sporadic*, create the false perception that there are few selected casualties. The general assumption was that the drone bombing was something from the past President. That's another angle to the lack of transparency. At one point, the lack of transparency on this issue was so evident that it was the Democrat-led Senate that had to take an initiative to force the White House to disclose at least some basic information."

Grandpa looked into his laptop and said. "I didn't prepare anything on this, but I'm sure we can find something." Then, he asked Grandma. "Could you find something on it?"

Grandma was talking with Mom and searching for something of their interest on her foldable screen, while Alice was doing her hair. They weren't aware of our conversation. She looked at Grandpa with a question mark like expression on her face.

"We've been talking about some other things here." But as Grandpa made a 'please, please' face, Granma said, "OK. So what is it you said you needed?"

Grandpa told her what we were talking about, and she quickly moved her fingers and in a matter of seconds she said.

"This is a piece of Los Angeles Times, published by Ken Dilanian, dated November 17, 2013. I guess this is what you're looking for."

Los Angeles Times, November 17, 2013[131]: *'Six months after President Obama vowed to change his administration's approach to lethal drone missile strikes, the pace of aerial attacks has fallen sharply, thanks in part to stricter targeting criteria.*

Obama also promised to make the drone campaign more transparent. But a blanket of secrecy thus far has remained firmly in place.

The Democrat-led Senate Intelligence Committee voted on Nov. 5 to require the administration to disclose how many civilians and militants were killed by drones each year. That tally has never been publicly available....

---

[131] Ken Dilanian, "Fewer U.S. drone strikes seen," *Los Angeles Post*, November 17, 2013.

"The American people should be given basic facts about mistakes when they are made, and they should also be given the rules that the government must follow when targeting and killing an American involved in terrorist activities," Sen. Ron Wyden (D-Ore.), a committee member, said in a statement....

Caitlin Hayden, spokeswoman for the National Security Council, said the administration already was transparent concerning drones.'

"Let me give you another example related to yesterday's oddity, Obamacare," said Grandpa. Then he added to Grandma. "Can you help us with the remaining research? I couldn't search for more data for this evening's conversation. You know, I spent the day out." And he put a pleading face.

"But Grandpa, what does transparency have to do with Obamacare?"

"Good question. There were at least two issues where transparency was needed. The first one being the Obamacare negotiations. Barack Obama promised to carry out negotiations in the open to show whether someone wanted to take advantage. Remember that there were several billion dollars at stake. The second one was implementation, as the implementation problems ended up impacting citizens."

"J.M., I remember there was a big flush on the negotiations issue," said Grandma, "and I remember a conversation with your aunt because she and her friends were looking for the televised negotiations."

"Are you kidding, Grandma? Negotiations on TV like a reality show? How did it go?"

"No, I am not kidding. That's why I remember it. Let's see, I am pretty sure the news reported it. Look." And Grandma pointed to the wall screen for us to read:

Barack Obama, August 21, 2008[132]: "I'm going to have all the negotiations around a big table. We'll have

doctors and nurses and hospital administrators.
Insurance companies, drug companies -- they'll get a seat
at the table, they just won't be able to buy every chair.
But what we will do is, we'll have the negotiations
televised on C-SPAN, so that people can see who is
making arguments on behalf of their constituents, and
who are making arguments on behalf of the drug
companies or the insurance companies. And so, that
approach, I think is what is going to allow people to
stay involved in this process.'

"Everyone on the same table? And on TV? That have been fun!" I said.

"None of it happened. They were never seated all together around the same table in negotiations, not even in private. There were no negotiations broadcasted. Although the Obama administration provided regular updates of their version of what happened behind doors, there wasn't any public records of the negotiations either."

"I could expect that much," said Dad. "I cannot envision all the players together on the same table, much less on TV. But, that's not a justification for the President making promises about transparency and how to go about it and, then, letting the citizens down. He should have known better."

"I agree. But, I think that the lack of transparency on the other problem, the implementation of Obamacare, was awkward," said Grandpa

"Do you mean President Obama saying in public there were no problems or that any problem had been resolved when people accessing the exchanges were suffering the *un-existing* problems?" Said Dad. He was no longer with his speed chess games.

"Yes, that's right. Users were entitled to know what was going on with the systems they had to use to register. But more specifically, there was one worrying issue, vulnerability

---

[132] Town hall meeting on August 21, 2008, in Chester, Va.

of private data at the Government exchanges."

"What do you mean?"

"Just days before the Internet site of Obamacare was set to open for users, a group of tech experts related to the Exchanges' implementation mentioned the lack of security. They indicated it was quite possible for hackers to obtain private data through the HealthCare.gov[133]."

I was shaking my head side to side, as if watching a ping pong match.

"And what happened?"

"The Healthcare Exchange went public on October first. The site was on the Internet as announced. Although it didn't work sixty percent of the time over the first months, hundreds of thousands introduced their personal data during uptimes. However, the security breach seemed to be there for a long time without any warning or other kind of official communication." Said Grandpa.

"And?" Dad asked.

"I didn't have time to finish the research today. But there were legislative initiatives, also supported by Democrats, to enforce the Administration to come out in the open with this thing." Explained Grandpa.

He then asked. "Grandma, could you help us and look for any bill asking the government to disclose security breaches on HealtCare.gov?"

Grandma was back explaining to Mom some of the things she had bought during her shopping spree.

I said, "Grandma, please. We need your help."

Alice interrupted. "I'm finishing your hair Grandma. Don't move. See? I'll get it fixed."

"About what?" Grandma asked.

Grandpa explained it to her, and she reluctantly changed windows again on her foldable screen and searched the information Grandpa asked for.

Once she found something, she showed Grandpa and sent it to the wall screen. We read.

[133] EdO'Keefe and Juliet Eilperin, "House approves HealthCare.gov security bill," *The Washington Post*, January 10, 2014.

The Wall Street Journal, January 10, 2014[134]: 'House Republicans on Friday sought to keep up political pressure on the Obama administration's health-care rollout, with the House passing legislation intended to address alleged security weaknesses with the HealthCare.gov website.

House lawmakers voted 291-122 in favor of the measure, which would require the government to notify users of the state and federal health exchanges within two business days of a suspected breach. Despite White House opposition to the measure, 67 Democrats joined Republicans in voting for the bill.

... House Republicans said the legislation is necessary to protect consumers from potential weaknesses with the HealthCare.gov site, which has been beset with problems since its Oct. 1 launch. They cited concerns raised by an official at the Centers for Medicare and Medicaid Services about security testing on the website before it went live.'

"The threat would probably seem quite real as a third of the Democrats supported the bill in Congress," said Dad.

I read aloud from the wall screen. "The White House opposition to the measure... what the hell! If there were no security problems why should they care to be asked to disclose security problems? And if there were security problems, they had an ethical obligation to be the first in disclosing such information without anyone asking them. I don't understand their game!"

"Oh yes, you do," Grandpa answered.

"Well, maybe I do Grandpa." I replied a bit sad. Adult reality wasn't looking that attractive to me, at least when it came to politics.

---

[134] Michael R. Crittenden, "House Passes Bill to Notify Users of Health Exchange Security Breaches," *The Wall Street Journal,* January 10, 2014.

Alice gave Grandma the mirror again to show her final touch. She looked proud of herself.

"I like it a lot, Alice. Could you add a queen tiara?"

"I'm going to!"

Grandpa was nodding in general to what we were saying, but his sight was suddenly lost somewhere else.

Dad brought him back to us, "Do you want a shot of that single malt whisky you liked so much?"

"Oh, yes, sure, thank you. I'd love it!"

Mom told Grandma. "Do you want tea or something? I guess you are going to help these two gentlemen" -signaling Grandpa and I with her hand- "with their searches. We can talk about the shopping tomorrow morning."

"Sure, thanks. Green tea, please," said Grandma.

"I'd love a decaf," said Dad.

Suddenly, Alice appeared from nowhere with a brandy snifter and said, "I want s'mores!" Then, to Grandpa, "Here you are Grandpa, you like whisky in these balloon glasses, don't you?"

"Thank you Alice. I certainly do. Single malt whisky in a balloon glass, without ice or water."

Mom went to the kitchen.

Grandma said to Alice, "where is my tiara, sweetheart?"

Alice was not hearing, she was insisting, "Daddy, can we make s'mores?"

"*Yes we can*," said Dad.

"Daddy, seriously," I said, "can we make s'mores? It's Friday..."

"Daddy, please," insisted Alice

"I told you, *yes we can*."

"I don't trust the *yes we can* sentence anymore! I'm emphasizing if we can have s'mores now?"

"Sure, I was just joking, J.M. "Why don't you bring some candles while I get the whisky."

Alice ran to the kitchen, "Mom, we are having s'mores! I'll take the marshmallows to the living room!"

A few minutes later, everyone had their drinks. The candles were ready, and Alice was piercing her first marshmallow in a wooden stick. Grandma had left her foldable screen and was cutting chocolate pieces. Both had forgotten about the tiara by now.

Mom asked Grandpa, "Dad, what about that large scandal around a guy called Snowman or Snowly or something like that."

"Mr. Snowden?" said Dad.

"Yes, that's a large, confusing and dark scandal!" said Mom.

"Who was Mr. Snowden?" I asked.

Alice interrupted the conversation, giggling. "Mr. Snowden's at the school playground. It's a fatty, round guy with stones for eyes. We made it this morning. It was fun!"

"Alice, come on!" I said. "We're talking serious stuff here!" I looked inquiringly to Grandpa.

He was concentrating in smelling his whisky. He always smelled it very slowly, several times, before taking his first sip.

"Grandpa..." I insisted.

"Snowden's scandal was very revealing. Not because of Mr. Snowden, but because of some of the reactions it provoked from the White House, odd explanations and behavior, indeed." said Grandpa.

He closed his eyes, and inhaled again the scent coming out of his balloon glass and continued.

"Before we get into who Mr. Snowden was, I think we need to illustrate some connotations of the word transparency."

"Here we go, back to your boring oddities," said Alice, taking her first marshmallows from the fire and choosing a dark chocolate piece.

Grandpa asked me, "J.M., is there any private information you'd like to know about any of your friends or teachers?"

"I don't know Grandpa. Kind of private what you are asking," I answered.

"Come on J.M., I'm sure you have some curiosities. It does not need to be unique though. Just something private you have no means to know."

"He would like to know anything about Ann Marie," said Alice mocking.

"Who's Ann Marie?" asked Grandma.

"No one," I said.

"She is J.M.'s girlfriend," said Alice, getting more interested in the conversation.

Dad was quite attentive too.

Grandpa said, "Let's assume you are interested in what Ann Marie does during the weekend, OK?"

Alice was enjoying the situation, but I did not like the way the conversation was going.

"I don't care what she does!" I said. "Could we go back to Mr. Snowden, Grandpa?"

"To continue on, I need you to tell me what you'd like to know about Ann Marie."

"OK, Grandpa," I answered with a tired voice. I thought for a minute and I made up something. I wasn't going to confide anything in public.

"I'd like to know what happens when Ethan goes fishing with his Dad. He always tells stories about how large the fishes he catches are. He never acknowledges his Dad is the one who fishes the large ones. He just shows us pictures of him with the fishes. But not taking them out of the water."

"Deal!" said Grandpa giving me a high-five. "So every Monday morning, I'll call you and tell you everything that happened with Ethan and his Dad over the weekend. What they've talked about while fishing, who catches which fish,-"

"And what about Ann Marie?" asked Alice.

"Forget about Ann Marie! Go on Grandpa."

"So, let's assume I brief you every Monday morning and you find revealing data you didn't know before. How would you think I've got the information?"

"But, do you have the information, Grandpa?"

"Just let's assume for a moment that I do get it before any briefing session with you. How do you think I've got it?"

"I don't know, you probably spied on Ethan following them on another boat, planting bugs..."

"What if your Dad asks you how you've got that information? If he asks you whether you've spied on Ethan, what would you say?"

"It was you who spied on him?"

"But how are you sure I spied on him?"

"I'm getting confused here," and I certainly was.

"If I don't tell you I'm spying on Ethan, you won't know for sure. You're making assumptions here. However, if your answer to your Dad is *'I don't know'* you are not lying, are you?

"I guess I'm not. But how else would you get the info?" I said.

Dad jumped in, "Technically speaking it wouldn't be a lie. It'd be a misleading truth, though."

"Indeed. So, J.M., if you answer *'I didn't spy and to my knowledge, no one was spying on Ethan'*, would your behavior be transparent?"

"As Daddy said, technically speaking I'll be saying the truth. But I wouldn't be transparent, would I? I mean, I'm pretty sure you did spy. How else would you get the info?"

"Grandpa, I'm making you a s'more," said Alice while chewing her own. "Which chocolate do you want, dark or brown?"

"Oh, thanks sweaty, brown chocolate please."

"Grandma, can you pass me the graham crackers, please? I'm making Grandpa a s'more!"

I wanted to get back to the conversation. "So, Grandpa, what's all this spying thing about? Did Obama spy? ...Of course! The President has all the spies working for him!"

"In 2013, when President Obama was on his second term, Mr. Snowden began disclosing thousands of classified documents that uncovered the presence of numerous global monitoring programs. Many of those programs were run by one of the U.S. Intelligence Agencies, the N.S.A."

"So what? By the way, you never answer the question of who Mr. Snowden was."

Grandpa looked at Grandma to ask her for help with information gathering, but Dad was quicker."

"I've got it here. I knew you were going to ask. This article summarizes who he was and what happened."

He sent the following text to the wall screen.

The Economist, January 4, 2014[135]*: 'Edward Snowden, an ex-contractor for the National Security Agency (NSA) now in Russia after exposing details of American cyber-spying worldwide. Mr Snowden's leaks have caused most fuss abroad. Brazil's president, Dilma Rousseff, called off a visit to America over reports that she was spied on along with a state energy giant, Petrobras. Politicians and the press in Germany, where memories of Nazi- and communist-era spying are undimmed, vie to sound more outraged about Mr Snowden's leaks, including reports that NSA spooks targeted Chancellor Angela Merkel. The European Parliament (a body whose default setting is chuntering indignation) is keener on debating the NSA than Congress is in Washington. Angered by reported spying on EU offices, various Euro-bigwigs have called for a pause in talks on an EU-American trade pact, as well as curbs on transAtlantic data-sharing.'*

I exclaimed, "Wow! I guess many people went crazy when they learned about what was happening"

"Some of the European and Latin-American governments had strong reactions to all this, especially allied governments. It seemed that the N.S.A. was also spying on foreign companies," said Grandpa.

"Certainly." And as Dad was scrolling down, he said, "Take a look at the next paragraph of the same article,"

Even friendly EU governments and officials are impatient for more robust assurances that America never, ever conducts economic espionage; talk of spying on Petrobras has jangled allies' nerves.

---

[135] Lexington Section. "Snooper blooper Revelations about cyber-espionage dismay Barack Obama's most loyal fans," *The Economist*, January 4, 2014.

"Petrobras, is one of the largest South American companies," said Grandpa.

"Yes, it's Brazilian. I remember that after Snowden started disclosing information, many countries, including Brazil, announced they were going to issue laws requiring that all internet companies should have their user's data in computers within the country borders and outside the U.S., to limit the espionage. Then, I guess they realized that those laws would be difficult to implement and wouldn't prevent the U.S. spying on their companies, people or government. Most of those laws were never implemented," said Grandpa.

"However, many large U.S. companies got worried because these potential laws from foreign countries would jeopardize their business abroad." Added Dad.

"Did Obama acknowledge he was spying on foreign governments and companies?" I asked.

"He maintained that he was being *technically* truthful, to use your Dad's words."

Mom clarified. "I guess it wasn't that easy for him to choose what to acknowledge, was it?"

"What do you mean?" I asked.

"President Obama was put in a cumbersome, embarrassing position. He had to concede that either he knew the N.S.A. was tapping into phone and emails of leaders of allied countries, or that, during his five years as President, spy agencies did as they wished without his knowledge. And as most of the surveillance programs started before Obama, it would mean he didn't have the command of the Agencies for five years. Strange though, because he received daily briefings from the Intelligence."

"I see, but did he know if his Administration was spying on allied governments?"

"I want to go on to what his reaction was as well as what were his following actions, because that's what I think is really odd. But let's cover this first. As we said, Obama opted for the technicality we've talked about earlier. So he didn't say, but some of his nearest collaborators basically said that the President didn't know. I'm sure there was plenty of coverage on the issue." addressing Grandma, he asked her to find any of these declarations.

Grandma sent to the wall screen a set of texts of which the first one had a comment by a top Senator and the President himself.

> *CNN, October 29, 2013[136]: 'President Barack Obama didn't know the United States was collecting communications of allied leaders such as German Chancellor Angela Merkel, the chairman of the Senate Intelligence Committee said on Monday.*
> *With the latest revelations from Snowden threatening to roil diplomatic relations in Europe, South America and elsewhere, the Obama administration maintained its firm and consistent response to all seeking answers -- we're not admitting anything, but we'll change it for the better.*
> *"I'm not here to talk about classified information. What I am confirming is the fact that we're undergoing a complete review of how our intelligence operates outside of the country," the President told Fusion TV.'*

Among the articles sent by Grandma to the wall screen. There were many saying that Obama did know. Several German newspapers asserted President Obama had personally authorized the tapping in 2010. Here are a couple of the articles Grandma projected.

> *The Telegraph, October 27, 2013[137]: 'President Barack Obama was told about monitoring of German Chancellor in 2010 and allowed it to continue, says German newspaper - President Barack Obama was*

---

[136] Tom Cohen, "Top senator: Obama didn't know of U.S. spying on Germany's leader," *CNN*, October 29, 2013.
[137] Philip Sherwell and Louise Barnett, 'Barack Obama 'approved tapping Angela Merkel's phone 3 years ago'," *The Telegraph*, October 27, 2013.

dragged into the trans-Atlantic spying row after it was claimed he personally authorised the monitoring of Angela Merkel's phone three years ago.

The president allegedly allowed US intelligence to listen to calls from the German Chancellor's mobile phone after he was briefed on the operation by Keith Alexander, director of the National Security Agency (NSA), in 2010.

The latest claim, reported in the German newspaper Bild am Sonntag, followed reports in Der Spiegel that the surveillance of Mrs Merkel's phone began as long ago as 2002, when she was still the opposition leader, three years before being elected Chancellor.

ABC News, October 28, 2013[138]: 'Obama wanted 'comprehensive dossier' on Merkel - Citing a source in Ms Merkel's office, other German media have reported that Mr Obama apologised to Ms Merkel when she called him on Wednesday, and told her that he would have stopped the bugging happening had he known about it.

But German newspaper Bild am Sonntag, citing a "US intelligence worker involved in the NSA operation against Merkel", said Mr Alexander informed Mr Obama in person about it in 2010.

"Obama didn't stop the operation back then but let it continue," the paper quoted the source as saying.

Bild am Sonntag said Mr Obama in fact wanted more material on Ms Merkel, and ordered the NSA to compile a "comprehensive dossier" on her.

---

[138] Michael Vincent, "Barack Obama knew US spies were targeting Germany's Angela Merkel," *ABC News*, October 28, 2013.

"Obama, according to the NSA man, did not trust Merkel and wanted to know everything about the German," the paper said.

The paper said the NSA had increased its surveillance, including the contents of Ms Merkel's text messages and phone calls, on Mr Obama's initiative and had started tapping a new, supposedly bug-proof mobile she acquired this summer, a sign the spying continued into the "recent past".

...Eighteen NSA staff working in the US embassy, some 800 metres from Ms Merkel's office, sent their findings straight to the White House, rather than to NSA headquarters, the paper said.'

"But, did it happen? I mean, did the N.S.A. eavesdrop Merkel?"

"You can't never say you're 100% certain when you're talking about Intelligence agencies. However, the documents disclosed by Mr. Snowden and the fact that President Obama promised the German Chancellor, Angela Merkel, she wouldn't be spying any longer, kind of acknowledges it happened, up to that point," said Grandpa.

"Grandma, could you highlight that paragraph of the Telegraph? ...Yes that one. Thanks"

The Telegraph, October 27, 2013[139]: *'Last week, however, Mr. Obama assured Mrs. Merkel that her phone is not being monitored now – and will not be in future. But the US has pointedly declined to discuss the NSA's actions in the past.'*

"So, you see. He didn't acknowledge anything. However, as Presidents are briefed every day on security matters, it is difficult to say he knew for certain, or he should have assumed the information he received came from

---

[139] *The Telegraph*, October 27, 2013.

eavesdropping. It is widely known that the daily briefing is based mostly on N.S.A. electronic surveillance though."

"But isn't it normal for everyone to spy on other governments?" Grandma asked.

"It is, however, the extent to which it was happening was what really amazed everyone."

Grandpa continued with his description.

"Eavesdropping foreign governments was one thing. Eavesdropping foreign companies was another. But the fact that *every* citizen in the U.S. was spied on is another matter that achieves a completely different level. The N.S.A. was collecting bulk telephone and internet communications all over the place."

I asked. "Are we all being taped? Do you mean if any phone conversation or e-mails are under surveillance?"

"In 2013, documents stolen and disclosed by Snowden indicated the N.S.A. was collecting information from all phones and many internet communications, together with webcams, private security cams and other sources."

"And did Obama know about this?"

"Indeed. He did. I'm sure Grandma will get the information right away."

And right to the point, Grandma sent the following text to the wall screen.

The Huffington Post, July 6, 2013[140]: *'President Barack Obama on Friday forcefully defended revelations that the National Security Agency is collecting phone records and electronic communications, saying that Congress was fully briefed and the programs are limited in scope.*

"The programs are secret in the sense that they are classified. They are not secret, in that every member of

---

[140] Luke Johnson, Obama Defends NSA Programs, Says Congress Knew About Surveillance, *The Huffington Post*, http://www.huffingtonpost.com/2013/06/07/obama-nsa_n_3403389.html (July 6, 2013).

Congress has been briefed," he said during a speech in San Jose, Calif. "These are programs that have been authored by large bipartisan majorities repeatedly since 2006."

"Your duly elected representatives have consistently been informed," he said.

News outlets revealed this week that vast spying programs began under President George W. Bush and have continued under Obama. The Guardian reported Wednesday that the National Security Agency had obtained a court order to collect phone records from Verizon Wireless customers, while The Washington Post reported Thursday of the existence of a program launched in 2007 called PRISM, which tracks information from nine leading U.S. Internet companies: Microsoft, Yahoo, Google, Facebook, AOL, YouTube, Apple, PalTalk and Skype.'

"Every member of Congress knew. However, it was a surprise to U.S. citizens," I said. "How could it be? That's astonishing!"

"Oh, I remember pretty well. Many people got angry when they learned about it," said Mom.

"What did President Obama do?"

"The fact that foreign governments were so angry and the fact that most US citizens, including most Democrats, considered monitoring everyone's phones unacceptable, he obviously had to act. A number of Democrats asked for the Obama's Administration to refrain from spying on everyone." Dad answered.

"How is that help coming along? Do you have anything about Democrats asking the Obama administration to stop?" Grandpa asked.

"Do you mean something like this?" said Grandma, sending the following text to the wall screen.

MSNBC, December 21, 2013[141]: 'Obama open to changes on NSA spying - Under pressure from Congress, the judiciary, and even his own advisory panel, President Barack Obama acknowledged that the National Security Agency's telephone metadata program may need to change.

"In light of the disclosures that have taken place it is clear that whatever benefits the configuration of this particular program may have may be outweighed by the concerns people have on its potential abuse," Obama told reporters during a press conference Friday. "And if that's the case there may be another way of skinning the cat."

... Legislators in Congress who had been pressing to end the NSA's bulk collection of communications data, such as Democratic Senator Patrick Leahy, claimed vindication. "The message to the NSA is now coming from every branch of government, from every corner of our nation, 'NSA you have gone too far," Leahy said on the Senate floor on Tuesday after the court ruling.'

"This MSNBC article talked about an advisory panel or something to review the situation. But I do not remember well. Do any of you remember?" said Grandpa

"I do remember. Appointing the committee and showing commitment to change the status quo settled up the turmoil among Americans. Let's see," said Dad looking into his phone.

After a few screen touches, he continued. "I have it here. In August 2013, President Obama asked a group of top US officials[142] to review US surveillance programs and to

---

[141] Adam Serwer, "Obama open to changes on NSA spying," *MSNBC*, http://www.msnbc.com/msnbc/the-president-willing-change-nsa-spying (December 21, 2013).

[142] Group of Officials: Richard Clarke, a longtime U.S. counterterrorism leader; Mr. Morell, the former CIA deputy director; Geoffrey Stone,

suggest a noteworthy makeover of both foreign and domestic spy practices."

"OK. So what *noteworthy makeover* did they recommend, Daddy?"

"Here are a number of major takeaways of the 49 recommendations, as compiled by the Wall Street Journal." And as soon as Dad sent the article, we read on the wall screen.

The Wall Street Journal, December 19, 2013[143]:
'Panel seeks to overhaul spy practices.

Major Takeaways From the Presidential Review Group's NSA Report:

The most notorious NSA program—its mass collection of telephone data—is not justified and should be terminated. The government should not hold such records.

An FBI practice of demanding information through the use of 'national security letters' should be placed under judicial supervision.

The U.S. should follow stricter privacy safeguards even when spying abroad, and should enter into surveillance agreements with close allies to govern spying.

The government should increase transparency by allowing telephone and data firms to tell customers when they are required to comply with federal information demands.'

"Terminate massive eavesdrop, put the FBI request under judicial supervision ...They do seem like recommendations that any President should have embraced on his first day in Office, I guess," said Mom.

University of Chicago law professor; Cass Sunstein, former White House regulatory official; and Peter Swire, a former economic and privacy official.
[143] Siobhan Gorman, Devlin Barret and Carol E. Lee, "Panel Seeks to Overhaul Spy Practices," *The Wall Street Journal*, December. 19, 2013.

"But, why wait until the scandal hit the fan in his fifth year as President? I mean, if he was serious about ethics and transparency, shouldn't he have changed the existing spy practices earlier?" I asked.

Upon reflection on my own words, I added. "Of course, if he didn't know about it he couldn't change the spy practices and he basically conveyed he didn't know, which is amazing."

Grandma asked Alice if she would prepare her a s'more. Alice was sitting on the floor. She got up to take some more graham crackers, and Laia, who was sitting by her, went over to Grandpa's side with her eyes fixed on Grandpa's s'more. But Grandpa didn't give her any. Instead, he offered Laia to smell his whisky. With a sharp retreat, Laia moved towards the other side. I guess she didn't like the strong smell.

I asked "But did Obama follow the experts committee's recommendations?"

"That's a good question, because his behavior was quite strange in regards to this." said Grandpa. "The Administration hasn't implemented or recommended any other major changes. The Administration was in the process to adopt a few of the minor ones while talking at length about implementing a major overhaul. But the adopted measures weren't necessarily those that meant to stop spying on every phone or on internet traffic. They also didn't increase the degree of information disclosed in a relevant way."

"Grandpa, you said that before, but I want to know what was done and what wasn't."

"Barack Obama gave some good speeches. There was a specific one in which he was going to announce the changes he'll make to the programs after the experts committee report. I remember it quite well, we were eager. However, I still remember the skepticism of some top journalist as the President gave his speech. Grandma, I'm sure there is still a lot in the Internet. It was at the end of December 2013 or in January 2014. Why don't you check?" asked Grandpa.

"Absolutely," said Grandma. We all looked towards her! She was now fully involved in the conversation. After she keyed her foldable screen she said

"Here you are." As she was reading aloud, we watched the wall screen with the following quote from Charlie Savage, of the New York Times[144]:

The New York Times, January 17, 2014: 'President Obama's promise to "end the Section 215 bulk metadata program as it currently exists" carries overtones of his promise, in January 2009, to close the Guantánamo Bay prison within a year. In both cases, has directed the government to do something, without providing a path to for how to accomplish it.

"This will not be simple," Mr. Obama acknowledged in his speech. He added, "More work needs to be done to determine exactly how this system might work."

... In the case of the bulk call records program, Mr. Obama is saying that he wants to get the government out of the business of collecting and holding all American's call records, but he wants to preserve the ability of counterterrorism analysts to search through up to two layers of call records, going back several years, for links to a terrorism suspect.

But, as he is acknowledging, there is currently no way to do this.'

"He promised something he knew it couldn't be achieved. Quite ironic!" Said Mom.

"Or so it looks," said Grandpa.

"At least he was truthfully acknowledging there was no way to implement his proposal," I said.

"Weird indeed!" Said Dad.

"And here you have another skeptic comment by the same journalist, regarding whether President Obama was, in fact, being transparent in regards to the surveillance of

---

[144] Charlie Savage comments, "The NY Times Live Coverage of Obama's N.S.A. Speech," *The New York Times*, January 17, 2014.

Foreign Leaders, basically what Grandpa summarized earlier to you with his metaphor," said Grandma, sending the following text to the wall screen..

> *The New York Times, January 17, 2014*[145]: *'Long before Mr. Obama's speech, the White House began reviewing its surveillance of leaders around the world — particularly its allies and partners. Aides to Mr. Obama suggested that dozens of monitoring efforts had been terminated, or stopped before they began.*
>
> *"If I want to know what they think about an issue, I'll pick up the phone and call them, rather than rely on surveillance," Mr. Obama said, gliding by the fact that leaders, of course, are frequently less than candid in their conversations with one another.*
>
> *Mr. Obama said that "unless there is a compelling reason" the United States would not monitor leaders of "friends and allies." He never defined who fits in those two categories. Pakistan? India? Mexico? Not surprisingly, Mr. Obama did not say. And he left open the question of whether the United States would spy on those below the leader levels — their chiefs of staff and intelligence officers and their military commands, among others.*

"Do you know what I remember from those speeches?" asked Grandpa.

Without waiting for a reply, he continued, "I got the feeling that President Obama tried to justify why he hadn't carried out any change in five years, on any of the spy programs he inherited from his predecessor. He was communicating he would take steps to correct it in 2014 because of his consideration to people instead because of Snowden's scandal. Why wait five years if he was so

---

[145] 'The NY Times Live Coverage of Obama's N.S.A. Speech"

convinced of the needs? That's odd. However, the oddest thing is that no major change happened after so many years and so many reassuring speeches."

"Is that true?" I asked. "What was the word experts used in the report? …Ah, yes, overhaul. Didn't Obama overhaul the spy programs this time around?"

"Well, I remember that the main discussion ended being not whether to collect all phone and internet traffic which was the recommendation, but whether the phone call information was going to be stored, inside the N.S.A. computers, or in a third company or in the FBI. The Administration managed to flip the discussions from whether they were allowed to collect data to where the collected data should be stored. The reason being that if the data was in another place, the Administration could say truthfully that the N.S.A. didn't hold information of all American citizens. And yes, the N.S.A. wouldn't, the information would have been collected anyway. Americans wanted to hear how there was going to be less of a privacy breach and not how data changed hands."

"But the expert panel recommendation was clear, the mass collection of telephone data should be terminated," said Mom.

"Yes, that was the recommendation but the President's speech conveyed the problem was about where to store data, not whether to collect the information in the first place. And as there was not a third party outside the government that wanted to store the data, records continued on where they were, at the N.S.A., and no halt to the massive collection program was envisioned."

"That is how I remember it as well[146]," said Dad.

"In his famous January, 2014 speech about the N.S.A. widespread data collection programs, President Obama said he'd been worried about surveillance programs and he had been taking actions during his five years as President to change these programs. Could you retrieve his speech

---

[146] As of the release of this book no final decision or legislation had been issued to change the status quo

Grandma?"

Grandma was savoring the last s'more Alice had prepared her. She left the last bit on a napkin over the coffee table, took her foldable screen and started to look for the information.

Before anyone realized what was happening, Laia was over the napkin taking the remaining piece of Grandma's s'more.

Mom yelled, "Laia! No!"

Laia jumped backwards and left quickly with the napkin stuck to her nose, and the s'more well in her mouth.

We all laughed.

Then Grandma found what Grandpa had asked for, and she sent the following text to the wall screen.

> *Barack Obama, January 17, 2014[147]: 'I maintained a healthy skepticism toward our surveillance programs after I became President. I ordered that our programs be reviewed by my national security team and our lawyers, and in some cases I ordered changes in how we did business. We increased oversight and auditing, including new structures aimed at compliance. Improved rules were proposed by the government and approved by the Foreign Intelligence Surveillance Court. And we sought to keep Congress continually updated on these activities.*

"This is what I was talking about. How could President Obama say he ordered a review of the programs when he became President and five years after that review was supposed to take place, he *suddenly* discovered that allied leaders were spied on without his knowledge. Obama left me wondering that day."

Dad interrupted. "Actually, it seems there were some symbolic agreements like the one reached in 2014 with technology companies. It was heralded as a great step, because the agreement between technology companies and

---

[147] President Barack Obama's remarks delivered on January 17, 2014.

President Obama allowed companies to disclose the broad number of information requests they've had from the U.S. government. But the agreement was achieved after a lawsuit to the Government by powerful companies and contributors such as Google, Facebook, Microsoft, LinkedIn and Yahoo."

"We could go on reviewing Mr. Snowden's disclosures and President Barack Obama's speeches and promises, but I think we've covered enough to convey what was so odd about the President and his relation with *transparency*. To finish up, I'd Like to show you three quotes I put together earlier this morning, before we went shopping. I think they summarize the message. Here they are."

TRANSPARENCY ODDITY
<u>Barack Obama, January 22, 2010</u>[148]: *'I'll never stop fighting to open up government. That's why we put in place the toughest ethics laws and toughest transparency rules of any administration in history.'*

<u>The Washington Examiner, February 14, 2013</u>[149]: *'During a "fireside hangout" on Google+ this afternoon, President Obama responded to a questioner who said she was disappointed in the gap between Obama's campaign promises for transparency and the reality of the last four years.*

"It feels a lot less transparent than I think we all hoped it would be," she said.

---

[148] Prepared remarks for President Obama's speech to a town-hall meeting, Lorain County Community College in Elyria, Ohio, January 22, 2010.
[149] Michal Conger, "Obama insists he runs the most transparent administration in history," *The Washington Examiner*, http://washingtonexaminer.com/obama-insists-he-runs-the-most-transparent-administration-in-history/article/2521644, (February 14, 2013).

Obama said firmly, "This is the most transparent administration in history, and I can document that is the case."'

[Author] Was President Obama talking about lobbyist hiring, drone bombing, or Obamacare transparency when he answered the above hangout?
Edward Snowden scandal broke out in June 2013.

New York Times Executive Editor Jill Abramson, January 2014[150]: 'I would say it is the most secretive White House that I have ever been involved in covering, and that includes. I spent 22 years of my career in Washington and covered presidents from President Reagan on up through now, and I was Washington bureau chief of the Times during George W. Bush's first term.'

"Wow! Barack Obama lived in transparency wonderland," I said.

We all read again the text on the wall screen. The transparency oddity was there, crystal-clear. Just in three paragraphs.

Grandma had continued surfing the net and wasn't aware that we just had finished when she said. "I have here an article about a well-known journalist from the Washington Post, expert in Washington matters. It confirms the whole oddity point plus he adds a factor of communication control by the Obama administration. Do you want me to show it, or should we leave it there?"

"Sure, why not. Show it to us." Said Grandpa

---

[150] New York Times Executive Editor Jill Abramson, January 2014.

The Huffington Post, October 10, 2013[151] *Obama Administration Has Gone To Unprecedented Lengths To Thwart Journalists, Report Finds*

Leonard Downie spent more than four decades at The Washington Post, including 17 years as the paper's top editor, and has heard plenty of grumbling from reporters blocked from access to government information. "I'm used to journalists complaining," he told HuffPost in an interview.

But after speaking to 30 veteran Washington journalists to prepare a Committee to Protect Journalists report, Downie said he was persuaded that concerns about lack of government transparency are legitimate. Those interviewed, he wrote, "could not remember any precedent" to the Obama administration's aggressive crackdown on leaks and efforts to control information.

David Sanger, chief Washington correspondent for The New York Times, said, "this is the most closed, control freak administration I've ever covered."

Times national security reporter Scott Shane said people in government are "scared to death" because of leak investigations. "It's having a deterrent effect," he added. "If we consider aggressive press coverage of government activities being at the core of American democracy, this tips the balance heavily in favor of the government."

Michael Oreskes, a senior managing editor at the AP, said, "The Obama administration has been extremely controlling and extremely resistant to journalistic intervention." Josh Meyer, a veteran Washington correspondent, said White House staffers "don't return

---

[151] Michael Calderone, "Obama Administration Has Gone To Unprecedented Lengths To Thwart Journalists, Report Finds," *The Huffington Post,* http://www.huffingtonpost.com/2013/10/10/obama-press-freedom-cpj_n_4073037.htm (October 10, 2013).

repeated phone calls and emails" and "feel entitled to and expect supportive media coverage."

Downie, who remains an unpaid editor-at-large for The Washington Post, spoke with several colleagues there researching the report.

Managing editor Kevin Merida said the Obama White House's "levels of sensitivity amaze me -- about something on Twitter or a headline on our website." Marcus Brauchli, the former Washington Post executive editor who succeeded Downie, said the Bush administration had a worse reputation" for transparency, but "in practice, it was much more accepting of the role of journalism in national security."

Post national security reporter Dana Priest spoke of putting less correspondence with sources in writing, given surveillance concerns. Cameron Barr, the paper's national editor, said "reporters are interviewing sources through intermediaries now, so the sources can truthfully answer on polygraphs that they didn't talk to reporters."

ABC News correspondent Ann Compton described Obama as the "least transparent of the seven presidents I've covered in terms of how he does his daily business."

....

"What I see here is that Obama campaigned against excessive secrecy, promised to have the most transparent government in American history, signed presidential directives in his first day of office with a lot of fanfare, continues to say in speeches and interviews and press conferences that transparency is a high priority for him, and it hasn't happened," Downie said. "It doesn't matter if he's a Republican or Democrat. It matters what he has promised and has not delivered."'

"Awesome," I said.

"I like the last sentence: it doesn't matter if he's a Republican or a Democrat."

"I'm exhausted, but I've enjoyed a lot! Thank you for your time and curiosity J.M." said Grandpa.

"Tomorrow you spend the day with me," said Alice.

"It's a promise."

I've never been great on hugs but I gave Grandpa a high-five and embraced him. "Great week! I'll have it with me all my life."

And I switched off the recorder function on my watch.

7 GRANDMA'S SUMMARY LESSON

Saturday, December 2, 2023 at 8:27 am

I woke up on a bright Saturday morning, nothing like the weather from the day before. The little snow that fell on Friday had melted away.

It was the beginning of the weekend which was great. But Grandma and Grandpa had to go back to their home on Sunday.

With those mixed feelings, I got up and put on my jeans and a T-shirt. A nice breakfast smell was coming from the kitchen that made my mouth water.

I run downstairs. As I entered the kitchen, I saw Grandma cooking bacon and ready to pour pancake mix over the pan.

"Good morning J.M. You're the first one to get up. How are you doing today? You look happy."

"Good morning Grandma. Yes, I'm happy. This week has been very interesting. I have learned a lot about President Obama. I will not forget about this week's after-dinner conversations with you and Grandpa." And I pointed to my watch to emphasize the point. She knew I recorded Grandpa's conversations.

"And what was your summary of all those hours?"

"Well, a lot of interesting stories I would guess. And that President Obama was not as good as some people expected. He was good in communications. But I understand also that Republicans made his work more difficult, though he had two years of a Democratic Congress and didn't achieve much either. What was your take away Grandma?"

Then she asked out of the blue, "J.M., are there any teachers in your school that the students fool around with?"

My parents weren't around the kitchen yet, so I laughed and answered.

"Oh yeah, Mr. Greenwald."

"And which grade does he teach?"

"Math and Science to 11th and 12th graders."

"Are all 11th and 12th grade teachers picked on by the students as well?"

"No way! You better not mess with Miss Hightoes. Students are fully aware when she's in the classroom! She can put you on the spot just for mumbling in her class and she makes it extremely embarrassing."

"J.M., here you have an example of what you may take away from the past five evenings. It is true that the surrounding individuals and conditions can affect one's ability to deliver. But Mr. Greenwald is fooled around by the same students that behave accordingly in Miss Hightoes' class."

She pointed to a chair for me to sit down.

"The lesson your Grandpa was teaching you was not a history lesson. It's based on history, but is a behavioral lesson: it is up to you to deliver results anytime you have a responsibility. You cannot blame the surroundings. On the contrary, he or she who has responsibility is responsible for managing around so as to achieve results. Mr. Greenwald can say that his students are unprepared and that he has no support from the student's families, or that the school class is too large. But Miss Hightoes is the living proof that he is only talking his way out of the blame for his lack of results."

"Very interesting point of view. I recall a paragraph in Grandpa's notes. He didn't use it. But let me go for it and read it to you. I think it is what you're saying."

"Are you sure? Your pancakes are almost ready."

"I'll be right back."

I went upstairs; picked up some of the notes Grandpa had left on the table the other day, picked up a page, and went back to the kitchen.

"Here I am Grandma, ready for the pancakes! Are you ready for a quote? It's from the Winners and losers article of The Economist."

And I read.

The Economist, November 6, 2013: '...It comes from Bill Clinton, who admires Mr Obama's policies—from his big health reforms to his stimulus measures, which arguably averted an economic depression—only to express sorrow at his insularity, his alienation of business and his distaste for the day-to-day business of politics. Mr Obama, observes Mr Clinton, "got all the hard stuff right," but "didn't do the easy stuff at all".'

"Certainly," said Grandma. "I couldn't say it better than President Bill Clinton."

"I've learned the lesson. I'll work and deliver good grades."

She laughed and served me her wonderful pancakes, sat on another chair and started to eat her papaya and drink a tea.

8 EPILOG

The difference between a candidate and a US President is that, the US President is the first executive of the Nation, the Commander in Chief as President Obama reminded in a good number of occasions... in businesslike talk, we could say he is the CEO of the Country.

And the difference between potentially good CEOs and really good CEOs is in execution, not in stating visionary goals. Lacking of execution in the business world end up in lack of results. And when they fail, some tend to cover the failures with a large list of "uncontrolled reasons", "enemies", and alike. Successful CEOs do have "Uncontrolled reasons", "enemies", and other external factors working against them. But they know how to manage them and take the time and effort required to deliver results.

Lack of execution is the expression that filtered through my Grandpa's speeches. Lack of execution not because the lack of good intentions, memorable objectives and high goals. Lack of execution through lack of management, dedication, negotiations...

It was not only my Grandpa's message on President Obama's mandates or my summary of our conversations. Many pro-Obama media and Americans got to the same conclusion during his second term. On November 2, 2013, just after one year of reelection, The Economist, a prestigious international journal that had supported Mr. Obama and his key program objectives, started its US Section with the article "Barack Obama's supporters are worried that he is a terrible manager". In this article, The Economist described an oddity as my Grandpa used to call them.

> *The Economist, November 2, 2013[152]: 'Whoops - Barack Obama's supporters are worried that he is a terrible manager - ... in two areas where he [President Obama] is unambiguously in charge -the Federal Health-Care Exchange and NSA- he seems bored by the daily tasks of governing and reluctant to question those who worked for him.*
>
> *.... if one part of the federal government cannot design and run a big computer system, how is another able to collect records of millions of conversations had by citizens of friendly countries and even snoop on their politicians?*
>
> *... Mr Obama's failure to make the boring bits of government work is infuriating, specifically for those that support his goals.'*

But what was really astonishing is that, in big scandals like the N.S.A. or problems in key issues like Obamacare, President Obama used to ask one of the most 'naive' questions an Executive could ask when it relates to the core of his job and to the information he should have: If I did know, do you think I would not have advised you? Do you think I would not have taken any corrective action?.

Odd indeed.

---

[152] The Presidency, "Whoops - Barack Obama's supporters are worried that he is a terrible manager," *The Economist*, November 2, 2013

A sound of soldiers getting ready, and movement around me as people opened their ceremony programs got me back to today. A day in which the US commemorates JFK's assassination, which is considered a turning point in America's politics and society.

Obama's Presidency was expected to be a much-needed turning point if you will in America's political history. However, he decided it ought not to be.

The conductor of the JFK assassination Commemoration Ceremony started to talk, so I finished my thoughts for the time being and drove my attention to the speaker.

J.M. MALIONN

ABOUT THE AUTHOR

J.M. Malionn has been analyzing and dissecting corporate, economic and trade markets for thirty five years. After traveling and working around the globe, he has settled with his wife in a little corner of the world, and he is now devoted to observing and sharing with his readers his observations.

The series of *Conversations between J.M. and Grandpa* are straight to the point talks on today's issues.